INTRODUCTION

In the half century since I entered the funeral business, much has changed. While the grief that people feel for the death of a loved one has remained the same, how we honour that person has not. One of the improvements, to my mind, is how we've personalized the rituals, most commonly with music, with stories, and with photographs.

The photographs are often the most meaningful. At a time of life lost, they remind us of a life lived. The joys, the milestones, the celebrations, the achievements, friends, and family.

When I started to write *From Paupers to Prime Ministers: A Life in Death—The Story*, I found myself going through all the old photographs and newspaper clippings that Hulse, Playfair & McGarry has collected since the firm was founded in 1925. They brought back a lot of smiles, some tears, but most of all, they brought back memories.

It struck me that these photographs should be shared, and so the idea for *The Album* was born.

Throughout my adult life, it has been next to impossible to separate my work from my family, my workplace from my community. Such is the nature of a family business—especially in the funeral profession. But I wouldn't have had it any other way.

The Album is, therefore, both a public tribute to Hulse, Playfair & McGarry on its more than eighty-five years in business, as well as my fifty years with the firm, and a private collection of photographs of my friends, my colleagues, my community, and my family, many of whom are one and the same.

They are memories of lives well-lived.

Brian McGarry

Prime Minister Stephen Harper and Brian McGarry discussing policy? Actually, they are discussing their daughters, Rachel and Sheetza, who are school chums. 2008.
Courtesy of the Prime Minister's Office.

Prime Minister Harper's letter of congratulations to Hulse, Playfair & McGarry,
as the firm celebrates eighty-five years of service to the National Capital Region,
and to Brian McGarry, approaching fifty years in funeral/cremation services.
Courtesy of the McGarry Family Archives.

CANADA

PRIME MINISTER   PREMIER MINISTRE

December 1 2009

Brian McGarry
Hulse, Playfair & McGarry
315 McLeod Street
Ottawa, ON K1P 1A2

Dear Mr. McGarry

I am very pleased to offer you and the dedicated team of funeral service professionals at Hulse, Playfair & McGarry my sincere congratulations as you celebrate two major milestones in 2010.

As a National Capital Region institution, your firm has provided comfort and support to grieving families for eighty-five years. During these decades of service, Hulse, Playfair & McGarry has earned a distinguished reputation for its generosity and commitment to the community. Your firm has also assumed a singular place in the commemorative history of the nation s capital, assisting in 22 funerals involving State Ceremony.

For the last fifty years, you have helped to guide the firm s commitment to operating as a locally and family owned funeral and cremation service provider   Inspired by the caring and dedicated service of your late father you have been a leader in the funeral services business. I know families across the Ottawa Valley have benefitted from your professionalism and kindness.

You stand as an example of how an individual can affect positive change and inspire a community. I know you have contributed your time, passion and financial resources to promote charitable efforts and events. Your good works have won you the admiration of your many friends and colleagues.

On behalf of the Government of Canada, I extend my best wishes for continued success.

Sincerely,

The Rt. Hon. Stephen Harper P C. M.P
Prime Minister of Canada

Long-time friend former prime minister Jean Chrétien, and his charming wife, Aline, chatting
with Brian McGarry about his forthcoming books.

Jean-Marc Carisse.

Former prime minister Jean Crétien's letter to Hulse, Playfair & McGarry congratulates the firm on
the occasion of its eighty-fifth anniversary and of Brian McGarry's fifty years of service, and for having
always remained a private, Canadian-owned, family firm and for its many services to the country.

Courtesy of the McGarry Family Archives.

Rt. Hon. Jean Chrétien, C.C., O.M., P.C., Q.C.
300 - 55 Metcalfe Street
Ottawa, Ontario K1P 6L5 Canada

January 2010

Dear Brian:

As your funeral/cremation company celebrates 85 years in business, 2010, and as you personally enter your 50th year in funeral service.

Aline and I want to congratulate you, your family, partners and employees. Hulse, Playfair & McGarry has remained a private Canadian owned Family Firm for all of these years. You have carried on the tradition of involving senior employees in ownership, serving Ottawa and Canada, caring for the total spectrum of Canadian society.

Your upcoming memoirs along with a pictorial album will match its title "From Paupers to Prime Ministers". I remember your involvement, along with Jean-Paul Roy from Heritage Canada, in the organizing of the Rt. Hon Pierre Trudeau's Funeral. There are many other occasions where you served our Country with State Ceremony: The Rt. Hon John Diefenbaker, Chief Justice Bora Laskin and the Hon. Stanley Knowles to name a few.

Very best wishes as you personally enter the next half-century of service.

Yours sincerely,

Jean Chrétien
Jean Chrétien

Brian McGarry, CEO
McGarry Family Chapels
315 McLeod Street
Ottawa, Ontario K2P 1A2

THE EARLY YEARS

Brian's mother and father, dressed in their "Sunday best," 1950. No, that is not their pleasure boat, only wishful thinking. Both were working-class people.
Courtesy of the McGarry Family Archives.

Unveiling of a monument erected in Wakefield, Quebec, in honour of Dr. Harold Geggie, a prominent local physician and Brian's mentor. Dr. Geggie's grandson and Brian's mother are pictured here. Late 1960s.
Courtesy of the McGarry Family Archives.

Brian's father, William McGarry, weeks before his death in a mining accident, with his daughter Mary-Ellen, age two, and sons Brian, age ten, and David, age thirteen. 1953.

Courtesy of the McGarry Family Archives.

The McGarry children, Mary-Ellen, Brian, and David, dressed for Sunday school. By 1953, their mother, Lyla, was widowed and left to bring up three young children on very little income.
Thomas Studio.

Christmas 1951. David, Mary-Ellen, sitting in her special chair, and "Cowboy Brian," who actually thought he might be Roy Rogers' son.
Courtesy of the McGarry Family Archives.

The Early Years ᵔ

Duck-tailed Brian driving his mom's '57 Chevy, equipped with fender skirts and bug screen.
Mom was not amused. 1960.

Courtesy of the McGarry Family Archives.

Graduation day, Canadian School of Embalming,
University of Toronto, 1964.

Courtesy of the Canadian School of Embalming.

Joe Hulse in front of his funeral home in Orangeville, Ontario. After receiving his early training from his Uncle Joe, Charles Hulse went on to become one of Canada's most prestigious and accomplished funeral home owners, establishing himself in Ottawa in 1925 at the age of twenty-six, when he purchased the Charles Woodburn Funeral Home.

Courtesy of the Hulse Family Archives.

Woodburn hearses, circa 1920.

Courtesy of Kristine Armit, Calgary.

Charles Hulse welcomes new partner, Brian McGarry, to Hulse & Playfair's
Central Chapel, McLeod Street, 1972.

Courtesy of the Hulse Family Archives.

CHARLES H. HULSE

TESTIMONIAL DINNER

A TRIBUTE TO 31 YEARS OF SERVICE

FRIDAY, JANUARY 15TH, 1965 - CHATEAU LAURIER

Very active in the community, Charles Hulse was once touted as a possible mayor of Ottawa. In preparation for the challenge, Charlotte Whitton floated the following slogan for her re-election campaign: "Ahead with Whitton or in a hearse with Hulse." Charles never ran for mayor; he instead supported fellow businessman Don Reid, who succeeded Charlotte as mayor in 1965. Here, Charles Hulse is honoured for his thirty-one years as trustee with the Ottawa School Board and eight years as chairman of the board.

Courtesy of the Kiwanis Club of Ottawa Archives.

Although Keith Playfair maintained a lower profile than his partner, Charles Hulse, he was also a very accomplished, affable, and well-liked man, whose social circle included many of the capital's elite.
Yousuf Karsh.

Keith Campbell, who became one of many employee-partners of Hulse & Playfair, leads the casket of Mackenzie King into St. Andrew's Presbyterian Church, Ottawa, for the state funeral service. 1950.
Newton Photographers.

The funeral of former prime minister Mackenzie King, as the casket departs from St. Andrew's
Presbyterian Church to travel from Ottawa to Toronto, where the former prime minister would
be interred in Mount Pleasant Cemetery. Charles Hulse, who conducted the funeral, gave each
honorary bearer an engraved silver cigarette case as a memento of the occasion. 1950.

Newton Photographers.

Vincent Massey ❧ 1967

First Native-Born Governor-General

Massey Dies in UK

LONDON (CP) — A Canadian government spokesman said today that Vincent Massey, 80, former governor-general of Canada has died.

Mr. Massey was the first native-born Canadian to become governor-general of Canada when he was appointed to the post in 1952 at the age of 65. He served until 1959.

MASSEY

J. E. G. Hardy, Canada's deputy high commissioner in London, said Mr. Massey died shortly after 10 a.m. (5 a.m. EST).

"He died peacefully," said Hardy, who added that Mr. Massey apparently had been suffering from pneumonia.

Death took place at King Edward VII's Hospital for Officers in London, where Mr. Massey had been under treatment for what until his death was an undisclosed illness.

Mr. Hardy said that if the former governor - general had been younger he might have survived his illness.

The first Canadian - born chief representative of the Queen in Canada, Mr. Massey was a front-line diplomat, expert on the arts and recognized throughout the world as in the first rank of Canadians.

SON AT SIDE

His son was reported in London with him when he entered hospital for treatment of what some friends first thought was influenza.

This was the impression that remained with his niece, Anna Massey, even to the time of his death. Britain is in the midst of a flu epidemic.

Mr. Massey served more than seven years as governor-general, from Feb. 28, 1952, to September, 1959. A governor-general usually is appointed for five years. But Mr. Massey was given two extensions, totalling about 2½ years.

Only one of his precedessors, Earl Gray, governor - general from 1904 to 1911, had been accorded two one-year extensions.

Before he became governor-general, Mr. Massey had been high commissioner in London and Canada's chief representative in Washington. He won national fame also for a report on the Canadian arts filed by a royal commission he led from 1949 to 1951.

Mr. Massey was Canada's first minister to Washington — from 1926 to 1930. He was Canadian high commissioner to London from 1936 to 1946.

He joined the Liberal cabinet of the late Mackenzie King as minister without portfolio in 1925. However, he was defeated in Ontario's Durham constituency in the general election that year and never sought elective office again.

Turn to Page 4—MASSEY

---

400 lansdowne road north
rockcliffe park ottawa 2

dear Mr Campbell

This is, I am afraid, a very brief note to thank you personally and your staff for all the help and guidance you gave during the three days following our return to Canada from London. I am very much aware of the importance of detail on such occasions and it was in great part thanks to you that everything went so smoothly.

With many thanks

Hart Massey

Hulse, Playfair & McGarry has had the distinct honour of assisting in state ceremonies for many distinguished Canadians, including governors general Vincent Massey and Georges Vanier.

Massey was one of the first Canadians to receive the Order of Canada. Mrs. Michener, Mrs. George Vanier, Governor General Michener, Vincent Massey, and Louis St. Laurent are pictured at the investiture. November 25, 1967.

Unknown / Courtesy of the McGarry Family Archives.

MASSEY'S BODY ARRIVES AT OTTAWA

RCMP pallbearers stand guard as a forklift vehicle lowers the coffin containing the body of former governor-general Vincent Massey from an aircraft at Ottawa Wednesday afternoon. The body was flown to Canada from London, England, where Mr. Massey died last Saturday.

(CP-Journal Wirephoto)

INSIGNIA BEARERS

Officers of the Queen's Own Regiment carry medals and honors of the late Vincent Massey from the aircraft to a hearse as the former governor-general's body arrived at Ottawa from London, England, Wednesday afternoon. Mr. Massey once served in the Queen's Own.

(CP-Journal Wirephoto)

Although state funerals are public occasions, each one is unique, as we work with the families to ensure that the ceremonies reflect the individual involved.

LYING IN STATE

Canadian troops and members of the clergy surround the coffin containing the body of former governor-general Vincent Massey in the chancel of Christ Church Anglican Cathedral Wednesday at Ottawa.

(CP-Journal Wirephoto)

A Quiet Farewell to Massey

Ottawa came to say farewell to Canada's first Canadian born governor-general Wednesday.

They came from all age groups, from all walks of life. They came to pay respects to Vincent Massey — scholar, diplomat, businessman, philanthropist, statesman.

FEW IN NUMBER

While in numbers they were small — only about 500 — they probably represented the feeling of people from across the land — a feeling of true sympathy and respect for a much-admired man.

They filed into Christ Church Cathedral, some kneeling in silent prayer, some walking past the flag-covered coffin, and then quietly left.

The coffin bearing the body of the late governor-general arrived shortly after 3 p.m. after its long journey from London.

Placed on a low carriage, it was drawn down the centre aisle of the near-century - old church.

A solemn procession was led by Ottawa Anglican Bishop Ernest S. Reed and Dean F. R. Gartrell of the cathedral. With the coffin were six members of the RCMP, followed by five officers of the Queen's Own Regiment of Canada carrying Mr. Massey's medals on a black velvet cushion.

Included was his final decoration — the Order of Canada — the new Canadian honor Mr. Massey received only two months ago.

GUARD CHANGES

The coffin was placed in the nave of the church and the first six-man vigil team took up positions. The guard, made up of army, navy, air force and RCMP personnel, was changed on the half hour right up until service time today.

First to pay their respects were members of the family: son Hart Massey, his wife and their son, Jonathan; daughter-in-law Mrs. Lionel Massey, wife of a deceased son and their three children, Jane, Evva and Susan; and a close family friend Mrs. Leigh Gossage.

They knelt for a short while and then walked quietly away.

Governor General Michener, accompanied by Bishop Reed, placed the Queen's wreath at the foot of the steps below the coffin. The wreath was made of red and white roses on cedar. A small card read simply "The Queen."

They stood for a few moments. Both then left.

Among the first officials to pay respects were Finance Minister Sharp, U.S. Ambassador W. Walton Butterworth, Agri-

culture Minister Greene and State Secretary Judy LaMarsh.

They were followed by Arnold Heeney, chairman of the Canadian section of the International Joint Commission and about 30 other members. Stanley Knowles (NDP—Winnipeg North Centre) was also present.

IN NEW UNIFORM

Then standing alone came Gen. Jean V. Allard, chief of the defence staff.

At about 3.45 p.m. the church was opened for public tribute. The first ones to come were students from a number of Ottawa schools and universities.

Shortly before 5 p.m. small clusters of homeward-bound

workers began to arrive. Leaving briefcases and parcels on back pews, they walked slowly down the long aisle.

Then came a number of area residents — parents with children in tow, military officers, groups of nuns, clergymen, older citizens — a cross section of the nation's capital.

Why had they come? For a number of different reasons.

VAGUE MEMORY

To a number of the students, the governor-general was just a vague memory of very early youth.

"I remember him inspecting troops once," said 17-year-old Cathy Manion, a Grade 13 Im-

maculata High School student. "I felt indebted to him because he was Canada's first governor-general."

Five co-eds from the University of Ottawa came because "we just wanted to pay our respects to the late governor-general and the office he represented."

Some of the older persons knew more of the man.

One lady, her hair almost snow white, said she knew both Mr. Massey and his wife "before the war."

'BRILLIANT MIND'

"He had a brilliant mind," she said. "He pointed out all the best in Canadian life."

Garth Hampson, his wife and two small children made a special trip from rural Ottawa to pay their final respects.

"He did a lot for Canada," said Mr. Hampson.

Another visitor, Denis Boyd, put it this way: "I think it was my duty to come because other Canadians didn't have a chance to. There are lots of Canadians who would have liked to pay their respects and there are a lot of Ottawa people who didn't take advantage of a thing like this."

Shortly after 9 p.m. all was left in stillness with only the six officers, their heads slightly bowed, standing watch.

FAREWELL FROM THE NATION

The governor-general led the official mourners, Wednesday, as the body of former governor-general Vincent Massey lay in state in Christ Church Cathedral. With Mr. Michener is his wife; Bishop Ernest Reed, centre, and Dean F. R. Gartrell. A constant vigil was maintained by representatives of the armed forces and the RCMP around the flag-draped coffin.

(Journal Photo by Dominion Wide)

Pearson funeral Sunday

Canadians mourn statesman-leader

By Ben Tierney
Southam News Services

Lester Bowles Pearson, Canada's 14th prime minister, is dead.

He died late Wednesday night, at the age of 75, in the quiet of his own home in Rockcliffe Park Village. The cause: Cancer.

Health appeared improved after operation to remove eye in 1970

In 1970 he underwent surgery to remove a tumor from behind his right eye.

It meant losing the eye, but for many months after the operation the former prime minister appeared to be in the best of health.

He made frequent public appearances in his work as chancellor of the Carleton University, in his association with the World Bank, and in connection with publication of the first volume of his memoirs.

About a month ago, however, he entered a hospital here with an undisclosed ailment. After a few days he was flown to Florida for what was to

★ ★ ★ ★ ★ ★

Recollections of a leader, tributes, pages 3 - 7

Mike Pearson diplomat, page 23

★ ★ ★ ★ ★ ★

have been a three-week vacation with his wife, Maryon. Then, the vacation was cut short.

He was flown home on Christmas Eve, to be joined by his daughter, Mrs. Patricia Hannah of Toronto, and his son, Geoffrey, a lecturer at the University of British Columbia.

He died within 72 hours of coming home.

Mr. Pearson will be buried with full state honors from Christ Church Cathedral at 2 p.m. Sunday with interment in a small cemetery near Wakefield in a plot he bought in the 1940s for $10.

His body will lie in state in the Hall of Honor in the Centre Block from 10 a.m. Saturday.

His death was announced by Mrs. Pearson in a brief note that was pinned to the bulletin board of the Parliamentary Press Gallery in which she asked that those who wished to pay tribute should make contributions to the Canadian Cancer Society.

Cancer reached liver

Earlier in the day, Mr. Pearson's physician, Dr. P. M. Burton, had told newsmen who inquired about the former prime minister's condition that he was suffering from cancer, and that the disease had reached his liver.

It was the first time that the nature of Mr. Pearson's illness had been specified.

Tributes to Mr. Pearson began to flow in within an hour of his death, and one of the first came from his old political antagonist, John George Diefenbaker.

"Whether in the field of diplomacy or politics," said 77-year-old Dief, "he was a happy warrior."

Wednesday afternoon, as the Mr. Pearson lay unconscious in an oxygen tent, Mr. Diefenbaker had hoped out loud that the whole country would pray that he would rally to health.

'Personal loss'

"I think I speak for Canadians as a whole," said Mr. Diefenbaker, "that their prayers should go up to Almighty God that He in His grace will allow Mr. Pearson to continue his work internationally, to which he is now giving his entire devotion."

Another tribute to Mr. Pearson came shortly after his death from the present leader of the Conservative Party, Robert Stanfield. He said:

"The death of Mr. Pearson is a matter of personal loss to me, as it is for Canadians of all political persuasions who knew him, respected him and liked him."

Prime Minister Trudeau, vacation-

ing near Vancouver, issued a lengthy tribute to Mr. Pearson within two hours of being told of Mr. Pearson's death.

In part, it said:

"The loss of the Rt. Hon. Lester B. Pearson is a great one, for men like him appear rarely. He was a man of ability and good will who worked in a greater part of his life to make the world a better place for others."

The prime minister called Mr. Pearson a man of international stature who was, first and foremost, a Canadian and who had "a strong faith in the final victory of the good forces of life."

"For the loss of a man of such faith," he said, "Canada is the poorer."

Life, career recounted

At the time of his death, Mr. Pearson was near completion of his three-volume memoirs recounting his youth, his days as a flyer in World War One and his years as a diplomat and politician.

The first volume of the memoirs — entitled, simply, "Mike" — was published only last month.

The second volume is said to be finished and the third volume complete as far as the year 1964.

Throughout Wednesday, as the hours moved Mr. Pearson closer to death, the street on which he lived was deserted.

The occasional car drove past his house, between the high banks of snow and tall black elm trees that lined the street, and now and then one stopped to deliver a parcel or a telegram, bring a friend or a relative, the doctor or the nurse.

But there was no gathering outside the white, two-storey frame house

---

TRUDEAU RETURNS TODAY

By The Canadian Press

Prime Minister Trudeau is returning to Ottawa from a Christmas vacation in British Columbia, and is expected to arrive here sometime later today.

The Trudeaus have been staying at the condominium of the prime minister's father-in-law, James Sinclair, in the Whistler area. Mr. Trudeau was seen only once in public Wednesday, by a group of anti-Vietnam war protesters.

Prof. Ray Bradley of Simon Fraser University was allowed to speak with the prime minister at the condominium and they discussed the war.

A CBC spokesman said in Vancouver that the prime minister's office had asked for studio facilities and air time here today for a nationwide statement on the death of Mr. Pearson by the prime minister.

---

with its black shutters, its upstairs curtains.

Even reporters and photographers, whose job it is to sometimes intrude, maintained their surveillance from a distance, out of respect for the man Canadians called Mike.

Tributes pour in

'Rare man' —Trudeau

(By The CP) — Prime Minister Trudeau said today Canada will be poorer for the loss of Lester Pearson.

In a statement issued by his office, Mr. Trudeau said Mr. Pearson was a man of international stature but first and foremost a Canadian.

The text of his comments:

"The loss of the Rt. Hon. Lester B. Pearson is a great one, for men like him appear rarely. He was a man of ability and good will who worked a greater part of his life to make the world a better place for others.

"Mr. Pearson was widely renowned for his genius and negotiations and diplomacy, for his very human qualities of compassion and quiet humor, for his major contributions toward peace and the welfare of man.

"He was tireless in his work on behalf of the United Nations which he called "our best hope for world peace'.

"He played a leading role in its organization and development, as well as in the work of its specialized agencies, and was influential in leading the UN to take giant steps toward

the attainment of its charter aims."

"These contributions were widely recognized: By the Nobel Peace Prize—he was the only Canadian ever to receive it; by Her Majesty The Queen's Prestigious Order of Merit—an order limited to 24 members; and by honorary degrees from more than 40 colleges and universities.

Turn to Page 4—RARE

One-eyed Mike umpire-baiter

TORONTO (CP)—Bryce Mackasey, a minister without portfolio in the Pearson cabinet, recounts a Pearson anecdote in The Star today about a visit the former prime minister made to a Montreal Expos baseball game.

Between innings he called the umpire over. 'You know, I've just got one eye,' he told him. The umpire looked embarrassed and mumbled something.

'You don't get my point,' Mr. Pearson continued. 'Even with one eye I can call strikes better than you with two.'"

'Lester was no name for an aspiring pilot'

By The Canadian Press

Lester Bowles Pearson is a relatively formal name and the bearer was anything but a formal man.

"If Lester is my name, Mike is what I am usually called. This change goes back to the First World War when I was training with the Royal Flying Corps. My squadron commander felt that Lester was no name for an aspiring fighter pilot and decided to call me Mike.

"It stuck, and I was glad to lose Lester."

January 9, 1973

Dear Mr. Lloyd,

    You have been so very helpful to us over the last sad days that I want to express my deep gratitude to you for your thoughtfulness and co-operation.

        Yours very sincerely,

Maryon Pearson

Mr. Cliff Lloyd,
   Hulse and Playfair Ltd.,
   Funeral Directors,
   315 McLeod,
      Ottawa.

Courtesy of the McGarry Family Archives.

In the melancholy Gatineau twilight, mourners trudge through snow to private burial at Wakefield cemetery

—Citizen-CP photo

Twilight farewell to Mike

By Dennis Foley
Citizen staff writer

Lester Bowles "Mike" Pearson, perhaps Canada's most beloved prime minister and certainly its most typically Canadian, was buried at twilight Sunday in a tiny Gatineau Hills pioneer cemetery following a rain-drenched state funeral.

A deeply appreciative country returned the body of its 14th prime minister to his family outside Ottawa's Christ Church Anglican Cathedral as army gunners fired a 19-gun salute and a solitary piper wailed the Mackintosh Lament.

The private graveside ceremony was attended by 36 relatives and close friends.

Before the coffin was lowered into the snow-covered frozen ground, the eight Royal Canadian Mounted Police sergeants who had borne it from the Centre Block Hall of Honor removed the Maple Leaf flag, folded it several times and presented it to Mrs. Pearson.

Wept slightly

The veiled Mrs. Pearson, who had remained stoically composed throughout the three-part state ceremony—the lying-in-state, the procession and church service—wept only a little when Very Rev. Arthur B. B. Moore, a long-time friend, offered his condolences at the graveside.

Close to 14,000 mourners ignored the worst possible winter weather Saturday and Sunday to pay their respects to the warm, lisping man with the puckish grin who always seemed to have time for them—schoolchildren wanting to be photographed with him, toothless old Indians in his Algoma East constituency, a neophyte newsman sheepishly approaching his first political leader.

About 8,000 people visited the wide hall on Saturday and another 6,000 on Sunday. Although viewing hours were extended to 12.30 p.m. Sunday, the main brass doors had to be closed in the faces of several people.

The visitors came in work clothes, formal dress, snowmobile suits and carried shopping bags and skates. Some were old; many were very young.

(The Funeral scene, page 29)

Sheetza McGarry learns about great Canadians from an early age. Here she spends time at the grave of former prime minister Lester B. Pearson in Wakefield, Quebec, where many of the McGarrys were born and raised.

Courtesy of the McGarry Family Archives.

Olive Diefenbaker ❧ 1976

Leaving First Baptist Church, Ottawa, after Olive Diefenbaker's funeral, 1976. John Diefenbaker, who died three years later, is at the top of the steps, accompanied by then president of Hulse, Playfair & McGarry, Cliff Lloyd. Corporate partners Alex Caldwell and Brian McGarry assist the active bearers with the casket.

Mrs. Diefenbaker was interred in Beechwood Cemetery, Ottawa, but after John Diefenbaker's death was disinterred and moved to Saskatoon to lie beside her husband. He felt the new location was more fitting. Note a young Joe Clark in the left front of the photo.

Unknown / Courtesy of the McGarry Family Archives.

FUNERAL OF OLIVE DIEFENBAKER

Died Wednesday, December 22, 1976 at approximately 1.30 p.m. at her home, 115 Lansdowne Road, Rockcliffe Park.

Dr. P.M. Burton notified Hulse & Playfair Ltd. at 2.30 p.m. Cliff Lloyd and International Funeral Service made the removal from the house.

Keith Martin (Executive Assistant to the Rt. Hon. John G. Diefenbaker) and Mrs. Betty Eligh (Secretary to Mr. Diefenbaker) met with Cliff Lloyd Wednesday afternoon to arrange details of funeral and to select the casket.

Maurice McGuinty and Brian McGarry prepared remains Wednesday afternoon.

On Thursday at 2 p.m. Mr. Diefenbaker came to the funeral home to receive friends. The casket remained open. Although Mr. Diefenbaker was not in attendance, friends were also permitted to call at the Funeral Home Thursday evening.

There were 44 floral tributes including: the casket spray from Mr. Diefenbaker, a wreath from The Governor General and Madame Leger; the National Press Club of Canada; many Progressive Conservative Associations; Premier and Mrs. William Davis; the R.C.M.P.; a number of Universities and the Ottawa Women's Canadian Club.

There were many donations to the Ontario Heart Foundation including: the Mayor and Members of Ottawa City Council; Mr. & Mrs. John McTeer and the Quota Club of Ottawa.

On Friday December 24th. the casket was escorted to the First Baptist Church, Laurier and Elgin Street, for the funeral service at 11 a.m. Cliff Lloyd remained with Mr. Diefenbaker and step-daughter Caroline Weir throughout the funeral; Keith Shaver attended to the Honourary Pallbearers, Brian McGarry attended to the Active Pallbearers and Alex Caldwell organized the movement of the casket.

Following the 45 minute service, conducted by Rev. Ralph Cummings, the cortege moved to Beechwood Cemetery where Mr. & Mrs. John Diefenbaker have a plot.

Courtesy of the McGarry Family Archives.

THE SENATE
CANADA

HON. DAVID J. WALKER, P.C., Q.C., LL.D.

29 XII 76.

Gentlemen:

You did a simply magnificent service from beginning to end in connection with the Olive Diefenbaker funeral.

Ottawa should be very proud of having such competent and refined people.

Very sincerely.

David J. Walker

Hulse & Playfair.
315 McLeod St
Ottawa.

John Diefenbaker and his stepdaughter, Carolyn Weir, leave the church funeral of Olive Diefenbaker.

Bill Brennan / Ottawa Citizen.

"The Chief." Brian had the privilege of meeting Mr. Diefenbaker many times. In his later years, Mr. Diefenbaker devoted much time to organizing his own funeral, the plans for which he called, "Operation Hope Not." When the time came, Federal Chief of Protocol Graham Glockling was instrumental in carrying out those plans—he was a real gentleman in every sense of the word. 1974.

Tsin Van / Courtesy of the McGarry Family Archives.

Leaving Christ Church Anglican Cathedral, Ottawa, 1979, during former prime minister John Diefenbaker's state funeral. As for Olive Diefenbaker's service in 1976, Alex Caldwell and Brian assist. With his back to the camera, Sergeant Major Eric Young directs the RCMP pallbearers—a true professional.

Unknown / Courtesy of the McGarry Family Archives.

John Diefenbaker ❧ *1979*

Amanda Dominque places a rose on Mr. Diefenbaker's hearse, which remained on the hood all the way from the church to the waiting funeral train for the rail trip to Saskatoon.

Courtesy of the City of Ottawa Archives / MG011/J79-1771B#12 / Dave Buston.

John Diefenbaker dead

Faithful 'McAndy' watches his master depart — René Pierre Allain-Journal/CP

John Diefenbaker: 1895 – 1979

Dief's body to lie in state in the House he loved

McAndy, Mr. Diefenbaker's dog, was confused as to why his master was taken away in a strange vehicle.

Can anyone identify the two fishermen in this photo? The first to do so wins a free lunch at the Rideau Club in Ottawa, hosted by Brian McGarry.

Courtesy of the Van Dusen Family.

John Diefenbaker ❧ 1979

Brian McGarry and Alex Caldwell. The final closing of John Diefenbaker's casket in the Hall of Honour, Centre Block, Parliament Buildings, Ottawa. Take note of the two flags joined on the casket: the Maple Leaf, which Mr. Diefenbaker had vehemently opposed at the time of its adoption in 1965, and the Red Ensign, which he had always championed. Another Canadian compromise.

John Evans.

Diefenbaker's casket leaving the Centre Block. Leading is Sergeant Major Eric Young of the RCMP, with family members behind the casket; Doug Kennedy, partner with Hulse, Playfair & McGarry; and finally, a slim Brian McGarry to the far right.

Rod MacIvor / Ottawa Citizen.

John Diefenbaker ✣ *1979*

John Diefenbaker's funeral procession leaves The Hill.

The Canadian Press / Mike Van Dusen.

Jules Léger ✺ 1980

Charles Hulse stated that he built Hulse & Playfair on two solid stones: the Kiwanis Club of Ottawa and the Ottawa Board of Education, to which he was elected for thirty-one years in fifteen consecutive elections. Brian has also had the great good fortune of belonging to Kiwanis since 1978. In this 1978 photo, Brian accompanies members of the Key Club, the youth branch of Kiwanis International, on a visit to Government House and Governor General Jules Léger (centre). Second from the right is Chuck Meagher, of Canada, world president of the Key Club, who was asked "a very important question" by the governor general: "Mr. Meagher, why does my prime minister [Pierre Trudeau] have an indoor swimming pool across the street at 24 Sussex, and here I am without one?" Chuck hesitated, then answered, "It must be, Your Excellency, that Mr. Trudeau has wealthier friends than yourself."

Tsin Van / Courtesy of the McGarry Family Archives.

Hulse & Playfair staff Duncan Lunam and Brian McGarry, just behind the hearse bearing the body of Jules Léger from Notre Dame Cathedral Basilica, Ottawa. Colonel Georges Bernier, chief of protocol, is front right. Behind the casket on the right, leading the honorary bearers, is Jean-Paul Roy, who succeeded Mr. Bernier. 1980.

Unknown / Courtesy of the McGarry Family Archives.

Three-day state rites set for 'remarkable son' Léger

By Regina Hickl-Szabo
and Rima Berns
Citizen staff writers

A state funeral is planned Thursday for former governor-general Jules Léger who died Saturday at the Ottawa General Hospital.

The body of the 67-year-old career diplomat will lie in state for three days in the East Block office he occupied more than 40 years ago as a member of Prime Minister MacKenzie King's staff.

The public can pay their respects to Léger on Tuesday in the East Block building on Parliament Hill from 7 to 10 p.m., Wednesday from 11:30 a.m. to 2:30 p.m. and again from 7 to 10 p.m., and Thursday from 11 a.m. to 1 p.m.

His brother, Paul-Emile Cardinal Léger, will participate, along the with the Roman Catholic primate of Canada Maurice Cardinal Roy, in the funeral service at the Basilica at 2 p.m. Thursday. Although the church only holds 1,200, more than 1,400 people are expected to attend the ceremony.

The former governor-general's death prompted an outpouring of sympathy from around the world.

In a brief message from Buckingham palace, Queen Elizabeth, offered her deepest sympathies to all Canadians, saying Léger was a "most distinguished man" who had "won the admiration of everyone" by fulfilling his duties as her representative in Canada despite a stroke in 1974 which temporarily robbed him of his speech and left him partially paralysed.

From Paris, Prime Minister Trudeau offered his condolences saying: "Canada has lost one of its most remarkable sons and public servants."

He praised Léger for "the strength of spirit, the wisdom and dignity with which he performed the duties of the high office of governor-general" for a full five years without succumbing to his illness.

Trudeau called on all francophones to be "especially proud" of Léger.

"They also owe him the recognition he deserves for working so hard all his life on their behalf."

His wife, Gabrielle, was at her husband's bedside when he died.

(Léger, page 33)

FUNÉRAILLES D'ÉTAT   STATE FUNERAL

Jules Léger
1913-1980

Basilique-cathédrale Notre-Dame d'Ottawa   Notre Dame of Ottawa Basilica
le jeudi 27 novembre 1980   Thursday, November 27, 1980

Courtesy of the McGarry Family Archives.

Unknown / Ottawa Citizen.

RT. HON. JULES LEGER FUNERAL

November 27, 1980
2:00 p.m.   *Says Pass for building*

Notre Dame of Ottawa Basilica

8:50 a.m. - Gagne take Shaver to Hill
9:00 a.m. - Gagne with #1 7pass. for Capt. Brule & Father Monet
9:15 a.m. - Staff meeting at H & P - McGarry
9:30 a.m. - Robert take McGarry to Hill
9:45 a.m. - Gagne with #1 7pass. to 20 Driveway for Cardinal & Mrs. Leger to East Block
9:45 a.m. - Robert with #2 7pass. to Four Seasons Hotel for Helene Leger then to East Block
9:45 a.m. - Mercier 7pass. and Hill 7pass. to Park Lane Hotel for Frechette & Dupuis Families
          then to East Block
12:30 p.m. - #1 Herse to Hill - Lunam
12:45 p.m. - Prepare casket for cortege - Shaver & McGarry
1:00 p.m. - McEvoy 7pass. to be in place on Hill for two honourary Pallbearers (see McGarry)
          Verify this car thursday a.m.
          - Also two additional McEvoy men on Hill 1:00 p.m. to help carry casket downstairs.
          Verify Thursday a.m. & ascertain how they are coming and departing off Hill.
          1:15 Gagne to château for Mrs Lapointe then to 20 Driveway
1:00 p.m. - Hills 7pass. to 1171 Ambleside Drive , Apt. 1710 (Ambleside 2) for Miss Blais
          then to 20 Driveway.
1:30 p.m. - Gagne with #1 7pass. to 20 Driveway for Mrs. Leger, Helene, Capt. Brule &
          Dianne Frechette, but wait for other three 7pass. to arrive.
1:25 p.m. - Robert with #2 7pass.to Park Lane for Dupuis Family then to 20 Driveway
          (probably four people)
1:25 p.m. - Mercier 7pass. to Park Lane for Frechette Family (probably three people) then
          to 20 Driveway
1:40 p.m. - All fou 7pass. to leave for the Basilica at precisely 1:40 p.m.; make way to
          King Edward Ave. North; left onto St. Patrick. (Police will be on intersection)
          - The order of this procession will be Gagne, Robert, Mercier & Hills.
          - Arrival at church must be 1:55 p.m. Slow down on St. Patrick Street if running
          ahead of schedule. Upon arrival at church pull up to St. Patrick door
          - (near Sussex). Have Families wait in cars.
          - X Gagne to inform Graham Glockling (or attendant at door) that families have
          arrived.
          - All drivers stay by cars; Secretary of State will escort families in and out
          of church.

CORTEGE FROM EAST BLOCK TO BASILICA

1:15 p/m/ (approximately)

          - Shaver, McGarry, Lunam and three McEvoy men to move casket downstairs. One
          McEvoy man return to Honourary Pallbearers' car; 2 McEvoy men return to their
          office.
1:33 p.m. - R.C.M.P. have moved casket to hearse
          - Shaver & Col. Georges Bernier to walk in procession in front of hearse.
          - Lunam and McGarry in hearse (see cortege plan). Check re flowers for top of casket
UPON ARRIVAL AT CHURCH   *Sise Phillean*

          - Lunam place carriage for casket.
          - R.C.M.P. move casket into church (Shaver at foot, McGarry at head)

UPON ARRIVAL, ETC. CORT.

          - Upon casket entering church, Lunam to return to office with hearse

Leading the funeral procession of Jules Léger through the streets of Ottawa are Colonel Georges Bernier and Keith Shaver, president of Hulse & Playfair. At the head of the two columns of cabinet colleagues are Jean-Luc Pepin on the left and Jean Marchand on the right. 1980.

Unknown / Courtesy of the McGarry Family Archives.

State Funeral
of The Right Honourable Bora Laskin

By Doug Kennedy
Hulse & Playfair Funeral Homes
Ottawa, Ontario

On the evening of Monday March 26, 1984, Hulse & Playfair Funeral Directors were notified of the death of The Right Honourable Bora Laskin, Chief Justice of the Supreme Court of Canada. Immediately, arrangements were made for a Hulse and Playfair representative to meet with the Laskin family and concurrently, the remains were transferred from hospital in Ottawa to Hulse & Playfair Central Chapel. Shortly thereafter the remains were transferred to the Ottawa Jewish Memorial Chapel. Funeral home personnel accompanied the family to the Jewish Memorial Chapel at which time preliminary arrangements were discussed along with members of the Jewish Chevra Kadisha (Jewish Burial Committee).

On Tuesday March 27, funeral

directors Keith Shaver and Brian McGarry met with government officials, of both The Prime Minister and Governor-General, R.C.M.P., representatives of the Justices of the Supreme Court and other related authorities. The service was scheduled for Wednesday March 28, 1984 at 11:00 a.m. with Rabbi Gunther Plout officiating. After

---

After lying in state in the Supreme Court of Canada, Chief Justice Bora Laskin was interred in Toronto, following a state ceremony at Ottawa's Jewish Memorial Chapel. To the right is Supreme Court Justice Brian Dickson, who later became Chief Justice of the Supreme Court. He was also honoured with a state funeral and then interred in a rural cemetery near his country home at Pinhey's Point on the Ottawa River. Brian McGarry remains a good friend of Brian Dickson Jr., an accomplished gentleman in his own right. 1984.

Unknown / Courtesy of the McGarry Family Archives.

the meeting Hulse & Playfair planned procedures and arranged for the necessary equipment and automobiles needed for the funeral.

The casket was transferred by Hulse & Playfair from the Jewish Memorial Chapel to the foyer of the Supreme Court of Canada at 7:30 a.m. on the morning of Wednesday, March 28. There was a lying-in-state until 10:30 a.m. and then the ceremony was initiated which was comprised of four different segments. They are as follows:

(a) A State procession from the Supreme Court of Canada Building to the War Memorial in front of the Parliament Buildings.

(b) A "breaking-off" of the official state involvement and a continuance of the procession to the Jewish Memorial Chapel. This portion of the funeral still included the Prime Minister's limousine, Governor-General's limousine and some 28 limousines including Justices of the Supreme Court, official honourary pallbearers and other invited guests.

(c) The funeral service at the Jewish Memorial Chapel at 11:00 a.m.

(d) The transfer of the casket to Canadian Forces Base at Uplands, Ottawa International Airport. The casket was secured in a Canadian Armed Forces Hercules Aircraft and family members, Hulse & Playfair directors and government representatives escorted the body to Toronto in a second aircraft provided by the Governor General. Both Ontario Provincial and Toronto police forces escorted family limousines to Holy Blossom Cemetery in Toronto for interment.

Steeles-College Memorial Chapel co-ordinated transportation requirements along with arranging the police escort and committal ceremony in Toronto. The interment was completed at 5 p.m. Wednesday.

It was indeed an honour for both funeral homes, Hulse & Playfair, Ottawa, and Steeles-College Memorial Chapel, Toronto, to be involved in the funeral arrangements of one of Canada's most outstanding Citizens.

Shirley Douglas places the urn of her father, Tommy Douglas, during the interment of the urn ceremony. Shirley's children: Kiefer Sutherland, standing second from left; Tom Douglas, fourth from left; and Rachel, not visible. At lunch following the ceremony, after eyeing him for some time, one rather shy waitress asked Kiefer, "Did anyone ever tell you that you have a close resemblance to the actor Kiefer Sutherland?" Kiefer responded by giving autographs to the servers. 1986.

Barry Schwerdfeger.

Tommy Douglas, with his friend, Stanley Knowles. Tommy Douglas, father of Canada's medicare system, became a friend of the McGarry family, along with his wife, Irma, when the McGarrys lived in Wakefield, Quebec. Their daughter Shirley, who lives in Toronto, remains a friend to this day. Shirley and the McGarrys visit occasionally and debate politics thoroughly. Stanley Knowles was also an icon of the CCF and later the New Democratic Party.

Unknown / Courtesy of the Shirley Douglas Archives.

Stanley Knowles's son David and his wife, Shirley, brought Sharon McGarry, Erin McGarry, and Brian to his father's parliamentary office following Stanley's death. Stanley Knowles was one of the greatest parliamentarians of the twentieth century, which his colleagues in the House of Commons recognized by placing a special chair in the House for him after his retirement.

Courtesy of the Knowles Family.

Courtesy of the McGarry Family Archives.

Stanley Knowles's casket entering the Centre Block, led by a young Brett McGarry, son of Sharon and Brian McGarry, who is now a lawyer practising in Ottawa. Prime Minister Jean Chrétien assigned a special area at the entrance to the House of Commons for the lying-in-state.

Mr. Knowles died during the middle of the 1997 election campaign, and Mr. Chrétien was on his way to Western Canada when he received the phone call with the news. Senator Joyce Fairbairn and Mr. Chrétien immediately instructed Hulse, Playfair & McGarry and State Protocol to recognize Mr. Knowles with the appropriate public visitation on Parliament Hill. *Courtesy of the McGarry Family Archives.*

The Ottawa Sun, Tuesday June 10 1997   Page S·

Legendary crusader for social justice Stanley Knowles dies at 88

'A great parliamentarian'

THE CONSCIENCE of Parliament died yesterday.

Stanley Knowles, a crusader for the underdog and one of the last links to the roots of Canadian socialism, died here nine days short of his 89th birthday.

He had been in poor health for years. He was diagnosed with multiple sclerosis in the '40s and suffered a severe stroke in 1981.

He was hospitalized last month with pneumonia and suffered a fatal stroke in hospital.

Knowles was one of the founding voices of the Canadian left, serving 40 years in Commons as a champion of the have-nots, gadfly to government and expert on the rules of the House.

Tributes poured in from politicians across the country of all stripes.

Prime Minister Jean Chrétien called him "a truly legendary parliamentarian."

Mr. Knowles was a very old friend of mine. He's been a member of Parliament with me since the beginning. I talked with him very often, so I'm terribly sorry."

NDP Leader Alexa McDonough called him "the dean of the House of Commons and the beloved friend of every Canadian whether they knew him or not. She said he served Canadians "with dignity and determination ... courage and vigor."

A LONG LIFE

Veteran parliamentarian Stanley Knowles died yesterday at 88. A sketch:
■ **Born:** In Los Angeles, June 18, 1908.
■ **Early Life:** Moved to Canada in 1924. Studied theology at United College, Winnipeg. Became United Church minister.
■ **Political Start:** Joined CCF 1935. Ran for Commons 1935 and 1940. Defeated. Ran for Manitoba legislature 1941. Defeated. Political Stats: Elected to Commons November 1942. Re-elected 1945, 1949, 1953, 1957. Defeated 1958. Re-elected 1962, 1963, 1965, 1968, 1972, 1974, 1979 and 1980.
■ **Accomplishments:** Instrumental in forming the NDP 1961. Made a member of the Privy Council 1979. Made honorary officer of the Commons, with permanent seat at the clerk's table (a unique honor) 1984. Officer, Order of Canada 1985.

And she said he earned his reputation as "the conscience of Parliament" who always treated the institution as "a reflection of Canadian democracy."

The prime minister said plans are being made for Knowles to lie in state in the Parliament Buildings. "We will honor him in a special fashion. I think the casket will come on the Hill."

The plan, yet to be finalized, would see the coffin lie in the foyer of the Commons on Thursday afternoon before a funeral service at a local church.

For Knowles, Parliament was a home away from home.

"You have given me a chance to live," Knowles said to then prime minister Pierre Trudeau who had just made him honorary officer of the House of Commons in 1983.

For Knowles, Trudeau's gesture was the crowning jewel on a matchless career that spanned four decades.

"Thank you, Pierre," he said, his voice filled with emotion.

Knowles had suffered a serious stroke a few years earlier, shortly after being re-elected for the 12th time in Winnipeg, where he first won a seat in 1942 as a member of the NDP's forerunner, the CCF.

He never fully recovered from the stroke, but Knowles became a fixture in the Commons, attending question period in the same chamber where he had de-voted his life to helping Canada's ordinary and underprivileged.

In an atmosphere generally associated with verbal attack and partisan confrontation, Knowles was the exception.

He was combative on issues that mattered to him and his party, but he always had the respect of his political adversaries. Long-time parliamentary observers agree Knowles made few – if any – enemies over the years.

Gov. Gen. Roméo LeBlanc said he "served his country and his constituents with distinction and grace," and described him as "a compassionate champion of social justice throughout his life."

Knowles, said LeBlanc, "contributed to the development of social policies and programs which we now regard as fundamentally Canadian," particularly universal medicare.

After his first election in 1942, Knowles lost only once, in the Diefenbaker sweep of 1958, until his retirement after his stroke.
— STAFF /CP

NOT FORGOTTEN: "Champion of social justice" Stanley Knowles sits in his honorary Commons seat in this April 1995 file photo. Knowles died yesterday.

FAREWELLS

Some of what was said on the death of Stanley Knowles:
■ "He will always remember his intelligence, his uncommon sense of public duty and his dedication to the ideals that first brought him to politics." — Gov. Gen. Roméo LeBlanc.
■ "He was a great parliamentarian and a great human being. I think I've lost a good friend." — Prime Minister Jean Chrétien.
■ "With courage and vigor, he fought incessantly in the House of Commons, which he viewed as very much the battleground for justice and equality in our society and deservedly won the reputation as the social conscience of Parliament." — NDP Leader Alexa McDonough.
■ "When the history books are written of this time ... people will say of Stanley Knowles that he was a prophet in the tradition of the biblical prophets ... calling the authorities of the day to account for what they were doing for the poor and the fatherless and the weak and the vulnerable." — Bill Blaikie, New Democrat MP for Winnipeg Transcona.
■ "He wasn't only a great student of Parliament and the rules, he also could quite vigorously in the area of social concerns. Certainly he was one of the great figures of parliamentary life in modern times." — Solicitor General Herb Gray, who served 20 years in Parliament across from Knowles.

BE SURE TO SAVE THIS CARD — IT TELLS YOU WHERE YOU WILL VOTE

— See the other side —

This information concerning the Federal Election of Monday, February 18, 1980, is furnished to you with the compliments of the New Democratic Party in Winnipeg North Centre. For any information concerning the election, call our headquarters:

1036 Notre Dame Avenue — Telephone 772-5795 or 774-1791

Mark Your Ballot With a Cross — X

KNOWLES, Stanley N.D.P. [X]

◆ OVER

Election cards and cartoon.

Courtesy of David Knowles.

WIN WITH THE C.C.F. — VOTE LABOR

For a PEOPLE'S VICTORY and a PEOPLE'S PEACE

STANLEY H.
KNOWLES   [X]

C.C.F. CANDIDATE FOR J. S. WOODSWORTH'S SEAT IN WINNIPEG NORTH CENTRE

Important:—There are two elections in Winnipeg this November. The Federal By-Election in Winnipeg North Centre will be held on MONDAY, November 30th, three days after the Winnipeg Civic Elections. Remember the date: MONDAY, Nov. 30th — Polls open at 8 a.m. and CLOSE at 6 P.M.

C.C.F. Telephones: 97 066 - 87 083 - 36 638

Andrew S. Robertson, Official Agent   Printed by Columbia Press, Ltd., Winnipeg

STANLEY H. KNOWLES

".. LET ME HAVE A LOOK AT YOUR PENSION PLAN!"

STANLEY KNOWLES 1908–1997

Thomas Boldt.

40   *Stanley Knowles ❧ 1997*

Reformer survives recount /2

WINNIPEG SUN

VOL. 17, No. 167   **Tuesday, June 17, 1997**   CITY 50¢   (OUTSIDE METRO 50¢)

'SAINT' LAID TO REST

Sun photo by FRED GREENSLADE

■ An RCMP honor guard carries casket containing body of S anley Knowles out Westminster United Church yesterday. See stories on page 3.

City hall averts layoffs, tax hikes

Finds $14M to chop from budget

It threatened to lay off 400 temporary workers. It considered a special flood tax on homeowners to deal with a projected deficit. Now, suddenly, the city is saying, never mind. As if by magic, $14 million in savings has been found, bringing the books back into the black. This leaves critics wondering why the cuts couldn't have been found in the first place.

PAGE 3

Sports

LEDBETTER LET LOOSE

Bombers boss Reinebold pulls another surprise /38

The funeral service and interment for Stanley Knowles took place in Winnipeg. 1997.

The paths of the Trudeau and the McGarry families crossed many times over the years. Pictured here are Kiwanians with Pierre Trudeau and Lloyd Francis, Speaker of the House of Commons (also a Kiwanian). Mr. Trudeau was very accommodating whenever we brought special guests to The Hill.

Tsin Van / Courtesy of the McGarry Family Archives.

Brian's sister, Mary-Ellen Schwerdfeger, her son, Tyler (now a funeral director), and Pierre Trudeau at a barbecue near the McGarry family's hometown of Wakefield, Quebec. Brian's brother-in-law, Barry Schwerdfeger, was the photographer on this occasion; he is also the chief-of-staff for McGarry Family Chapel's cremation operations. 1980. *Barry Schwerdfeger.*

Brian's brother and sister-in-law, David and Kilby McGarry. *Barry Schwerdfeger.*

In Pierre Trudeau's office with Key Club visitors, along with Lloyd Francis (who served as Speaker of the House in 1984) and Brian on the right. Pierre Trudeau is holding a sparkling new golden ruler given to him by the Key Club. Metric measurement had recently been introduced in Canada. 1976.

Tsin Van / Courtesy of the McGarry Family Archives.

Taking a break at RCMP headquarters in Ottawa. To Brian's left is Hulse, Playfair & McGarry employee-partner Don Renaud, who was instrumental in organizing Mr. Trudeau's funeral on behalf of the firm. To Don's left is Brian's brother-in-law, Barry Schwerdfeger. To his left is Debbie Reitenback, who was in charge of RCMP pallbearers.

Courtesy of the Royal Canadian Mounted Police.

Margaret Trudeau, with her sons Justin on her right and Sacha on her left, observing Pierre Trudeau's casket arriving on Parliament Hill. Thousands upon thousands of Canadians came out to The Hill to pay their respects, forcing funeral organizers to keep the Centre Block open until three o clock in the morning.

To the far left is Patrick McGarry, often mistaken for Sharon and Brian's son, Brett. Patrick is now the Chief Operating Officer of McGarry Family Chapels.

Jean-Marc Carisse.

The casket of Pierre Trudeau leaving the Hall of Honour and the lying-in-state at Parliament Hill, followed by Justin and Sacha Trudeau, Prime Minister and Mrs. Chrétien, and many dignitaries. To the right in the photo, just to Brian's side, is Stockwell Day, then Leader of the Opposition, and in the foreground, Deputy Prime Minister Herb Gray.

Jean-Marc Carisse.

Mr. Trudeau's funeral train to Montreal made many stops en route as thousands of Canadians gathered at railway crossings to pay tribute with flags and applause.
André Gagné.

Despite a bomb threat, the visitation at Montreal's city hall and mass at Notre Dame Church proceeded with absolute dignity and precision. Justin Trudeau delivered a rivetting eulogy. World leaders in attendance included former U.S. president Jimmy Carter, Fidel Castro of Cuba, and Prince Andrew, who is not in this photo. To Mr. Carter's right is Jean-Marc Lalonde, cabinet minister and confidant to Pierre Trudeau. *The Canadian Press / Adrian Wyld.*

Among the McGarrys' favourite vice-regal couples are Ray and Gerda Hnatyshyn. Here they welcome
Sharon McGarry and Brian to Government House in 1990. In a previous career at Gowlings law
firm, Sharon worked with Ray before he became governor general. Brian first met Ray during John
Diefenbaker's funeral in 1979, where he was an honorary pallbearer. One could not help but immediately
like this gentle man and his wife, Gerda.

Courtesy of Government House.

Ray and Gerda at the funeral of Supreme Court Justice John Sopinka. Directly behind Gerda is Ottawa lawyer Richard Dearden, friend of the Hnatyshyns, John Sopinka, and the McGarrys, and most important to Brian, supporter of all of his political campaigns, some more successful than others. 1997.

Unknown / Courtesy of the McGarry Family Archives.

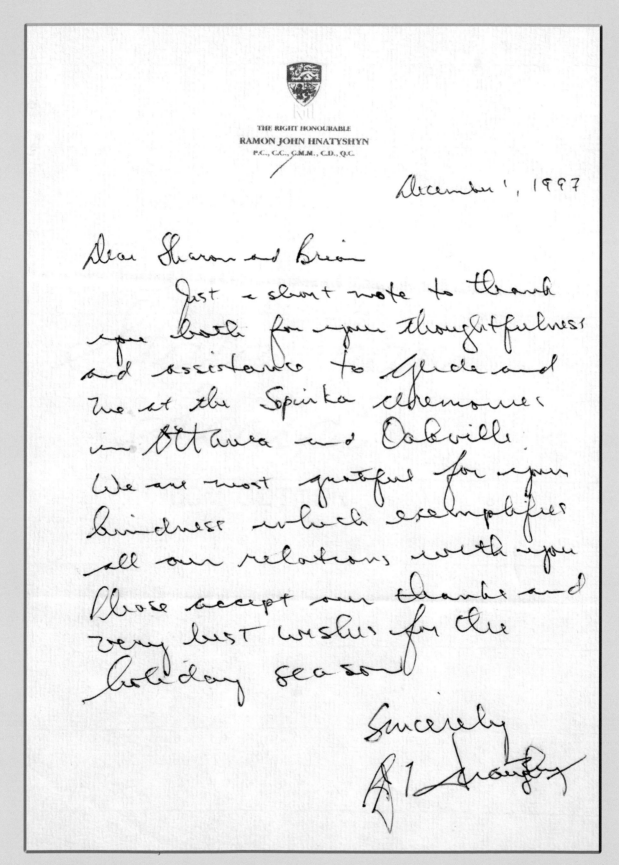

THE RIGHT HONOURABLE
RAMON JOHN HNATYSHYN
P.C., C.C., C.M.M., C.D., Q.C.

December 1, 1997

Dear Sharon and Brian

Just a short note to thank you both for your thoughtfulness and assistance to Gerda and me at the Spirka ceremonies in Ottawa and Oakville. We are most grateful for your kindness which exemplifies all our relations with you. Please accept our thanks and very best wishes for the holiday season.

Sincerely

A friend takes the time to write. *Courtesy of the McGarry Family Archives.*

A quintessential Canadian

Amid the ancient rites to mark the passing of a former governor general, there were laughs, joyous memories and tales of vice-regal silliness. Ray Hnatyshyn, always a man of the people, would have wanted it that way, writes **Randy Boswell**.

A slow, mournful procession of dark horses, black limousines and grim-faced soldiers. Sombre priests. Tearful friends. A bitter December wind whipping through the streets of Ottawa.

And hearty chuckles. Punchlines. High jinks and hilarity. Tales of vice-regal silliness of the highest order.

It was a state funeral like no other, an amalgam of ancient rituals of grief to mark the death of Ray Hnatyshyn, and heartfelt expressions of joy over the former governor general's legacy of laughter, public service and universal respect.

Mr. Hnatyshyn, 68, a Saskatchewan lawyer who rose to become federal justice minister in the Conservative government of Brian Mulroney, died on Wednesday of complications from pancreatitis.

His political defeat in 1988, ironically, cleared the way for a return to Ottawa in 1990 as governor general, a post he held until 1995.

During his time as Canada's de facto head of state, Mr. Hnatyshyn refashioned the role in his own image, re-admitting the public to what had become a cloistered Rideau Hall and leavening the traditional stiffness of vice-regality with public bursts of laughter and a Prairie boy's natural warmth.

Had he been alive to witness the elaborate ceremony surrounding his sendoff yesterday, Mr. Hnatyshyn would have been "cracking jokes" and "finding the formality of the occasion a little bit odd," said friend and former federal cabinet colleague Perrin Beatty.

"He was the most informal person going."

And so we learned during a funeral service that was punctuated by laughter. Among those in attendance were Prime Minister Jean Chrétien and two of his Tory predecessors, Joe Clark and Kim Campbell, as well as former governor general Roméo LeBlanc, Supreme Court Chief Justice Beverley McLachlin and a host of Mr. Hnatyshyn's former political colleagues.

When CBC television news anchor Peter Mansbridge offered the "Wine Anecdote" during the eulogy for his lost friend and golfing buddy, it was indeed a testament to the fact that Mr. Hnatyshyn "would really do almost anything to get a laugh."

Mr. Mansbridge recalled a dinner out with a group of friends. Mr. Hnatyshyn, who had shared meals with the Queen and a host of world leaders during his days at Rideau Hall, accepted a waiter's offer to taste the wine.

Suddenly, Mr. Hnatyshyn gagged, grabbed for his throat.

BRIGITTE BOUVIER, THE OTTAWA CITIZEN

ROD MACIVOR, THE OTTAWA CITIZEN

Top: Ray Hnatyshyn's family — from left to right, his son John, his daughter-in-law Marisa Fusaro, his widow Gerda, and his son Carl — watch as the former governor general's casket is take from the Centre Block for his funeral at Christ Church Cathedral. Above, Prime Minister Jean Chrétien greets former prime minister Kim Campbell on the steps of the church.

BRIGITTE BOUVIER, THE OTTAWA CITIZEN

John and Carl Hnatyshyn follow the flag-draped casket of their father, former governor general Ray Hnatyshyn, as it leaves Parliament Hill after a two-day lying in state. Pallbearers from the Governor General's Foot Guards escorted the casket to Christ Church Cathedral.

ROD MACIVOR, THE OTTAWA CITIZEN   ROD MACIVOR, THE OTTAWA CITIZEN   ROD MACIVOR, THE OTTAWA CITIZEN

ROD MACIVOR, THE OTTAWA CITIZEN   ROD MACIVOR, THE OTTAWA CITIZEN   BRIGITTE BOUVIER, OTTAWA CITIZEN

Among the dignitaries and politicians attending yesterday's funeral, were, clockwise from top left: Supreme Court Chief Justice Beverley McLachlin, Ontario Lt. Gov. James Bartleman, former Tory cabinet ministers Flora MacDonald, Don Mazankowski and Barbara McDougall, and former governor general Roméo LeBlanc.

A man for all Canadians, Ray Hnatyshyn leaves the lying-in-state, which was held in the Senate Chamber, then down the steps from the Centre Block. In a gracious gesture, Gerda Hnatyshyn and her sons, John and Karl, insisted that the Christmas decorations inside the Centre Block not be removed. Gerda felt that the seasonal festivities should carry on.

Leading the casket is Terry Christopher, a dignified, friendly man who served as Usher of the Black Rod of the Senate. To the left at the top of the steps is Sharon McGarry assisting the Hnatyshyn family.

The Right Honourable Ramon Hnatyshyn leaving The Hill for the last time, where he served
Canada first as an MP, and then as governor general.

Jean Levac / Ottawa Citizen.

Mr. Hnatyshyn's casket making its way from Parliament Hill to Christ Church Cathedral,
Ottawa. At the left front corner is Kevin MacLeod, Chief of Protocol at the time. Kevin is now
the Usher of the Black Rod of the Senate of Canada and Canadian Secretary to the Queen. Kevin
was among the finest when it came to state protocol.

Jean Levac / Ottawa Citizen.

 **Canadian Heritage**   Patrimoine canadien

January 4, 2003

Mr. Brian McGarry
Chief Executive Officer
Hulse, Plairfair and McGarry
315 McLeod Street
Ottawa, Ontario
K2P 1A2

Dear Brian:

I am simply writing to express the most sincere thanks of the Department of Canadian Heritage, and by extension the Government of Canada, for Hulse, Playfair and McGarry's involvement in the lying in state and state funeral for the late The Right Honourable Ramon John Hnatyshyn.

Those six days were a very intense and sometimes stressful time for the Canadian Heritage personnel who were called upon to oversee the execution of these events. However, the consummate professionalism of your company and staff made our task at hand much more bearable. Your attention to detail and vigilance in the execution of every movement ensured that everything went according to plan. In this regard, I would be most grateful if our special thanks could be extended to Sharon, Donald and Tom who were truly a pleasure to deal with throughout.

Now, with the passage of two weeks, I have had an opportunity to reflect on both the nature and delivery of both the lying in state and the state funeral. I firmly believe that, collectively, we have contributed to delivering these events in a manner befitting the man who we all so admired.

Once again Brian, our grateful thanks to you and the entire Hulse, Playfair and McGarry team for your sage advice, solid support and incredible professionalism at every stage. It was greatly appreciated by us all. With all good wishes for a happy, healthy and prosperous 2003, I remain

Sincerely,

Kevin MacLeod
Manager
State Ceremonial and Protcol

Canadä

Chief Justice Antonio Lamer, one of Canada's longest-serving federal judges, who spent nearly twenty years on the Supreme Court, half of them as chief justice. Following the lying-in-state at the Supreme Court of Canada, a funeral service took place in Montreal. Pictured at far right, behind the casket, is one of Brian's most trusted former partners, André Robert.

The Canadian Press / Ryan Remoirz.

RCMP pallbearers bringing Jack Layton's casket into the Centre Block for the lying-in-state. While state funerals are generally reserved for sitting and past prime ministers, sitting and past governors general, and sitting and past chief justices of the Supreme Court of Canada, Prime Minister Stephen Harper offered a state funeral for Jack Layton, Leader of the Official Opposition, who died in office, which Jack's widow, Olivia, accepted. Rosar-Morrison Funeral Home of Toronto led the funeral directors, supplying a supportive role. *Jean-Marc Carisse.*

Sheetza McGarry assisting her dad as her brother, Brett, did with Stanley Knowles, fourteen years before.
Jean-Marc Carisse.

Jack Layton lying-in-state, Commons Entrance, where NDP icon Stanley Knowles also lay in state in 1997.

Jean-Marc Carisse.

Olivia Chow
leaving The Hill.
Jean-Marc Carisse.

Laureen Harper paying her respects to Jack Layton before speaking to Jack's wife, Olivia Chow.
Jean-Marc Carisse.

Jack Layton's family on the steps of the Centre Block, from left to right: wife Olivia Chow, granddaughter Beatrice, son-in-law Hugh Campbell, daughter Sarah, son Michael.

Jean-Marc Carisse.

Malak
PHOTOGRAPHS LIMITED

Publicity • Industrial • Commercial • 37 First Avenue, Ottawa, Ontario, Canada K1S 2G1 • Tel. (613) 235-1884
FAX: (613) 235-1891

November 17, 2001

Mr. Brian McGarry
Chief Executive Officer
Hulse, Playfair & McGarry
315 McLeod Street
Ottawa, Ontario
K1P 1A2

Dear Mr. McGarry:

Thank you for arranging and managing my husband's funeral with so much
professionalism and dignity. Your team, especially Sharon McGarry and
Mr. Tom Flood were most responsive to our needs on this very sad occasion.

I would also like to thank you for your hospitality and generosity provided to
us in Wakefield. It was wonderful to have a venue to get together with family
and friends in such a beautiful location.

Yours sincerely,

Barbara Karsh

Courtesy of the McGarry Family Archives.

THE OTTAWA CITIZEN SECTION C

CITY

Arts: page C7

Classified: page C11

Long lost son finally comes home

Adopted son of former Chelsea mayor finds his mother after 41 years. C3

Malak Karsh 'had a smile for everyone'

Beloved photographer and founder of tulip festival buried in Wakefield

BY RANDY BOSWELL

A "grateful" immigrant Canadian whose patriotism was unsurpassed.

A "truly gentle" family man with "no temper," "no enemies" and a smile for everyone — "regardless of age, position or heritage."

A visionary who would become the national capital's "greatest ambassador."

An "inspired" and "driven" artist who created a unique "photographic monument" for eternity but whom "wealth steadfastly eluded."

Amid much laughter and more than a few tears, they celebrated the life and mourned the loss of photographer Malak Karsh yesterday, in a downtown church just large enough for the 300 who paid tribute to Ottawa's prolific master of the sublime.

The steps to St. John the Evangelist Anglican Church were lined with 32 pots of bright red tulips — the flower which through photographs won Malak his fame — flown in specially from the Netherlands following word of his passing. The casket, upon which a velvety pillow lay bearing his Order of Canada medal, was placed near the altar and flanked by two massive vessels filled with white tulips — one sent from Boston by his ailing older brother Yousuf, the world famous portrait photographer who helped launch the younger Karsh's career.

Malak, 86, had been battling leukemia before his death on Thursday. And yet despite his illness and advanced years, friends and family who spoke at the funeral said they were still struggling to accept the loss of a man who seemed to define dynamism and defy nature — even as he made its glorification his life's work.

Again and again there were stories of a grey-haired fellow seen scrambling about town with his cameras and trademark stepladder — on Parliament Hill, in the woods, in tulip beds, in knee-deep snow — straining for just the right angle to flatter his myriad subjects.

There was a retelling of the wonderful tale of Malak's epiphanic trip to Gatineau Park in 1937, the year he came to Canada from Armenia to work with Yousuf. One glimpse of a flaming red fall scene, just minutes from the heart of Ottawa, would spark a 60-year-career in which Malak sought to capture the essential beauty of a nation and its capital.

The sea of postcards, calendars and coffee table books bearing Malak's images of Ottawa and Canada are a testament to the success of his photographic mission.

"There are very few Canadians who are as proud of their country as he was," said Marcel Beaudry, chairman of the National Capital Commission, in one of several remembrances given at the funeral. "His talents and his passion are what made him great, his warmth and kindness are what made him a great Canadian.... We can find comfort in our memories and his great works."

A past NCC chairwoman,

DAVE CHAN, THE OTTAWA CITIZEN

About 300 people gathered for the funeral for Malak Karsh yesterday, held at St. John the Evangelist Anglican Church. Among the high-profile citizens in attendance were Jean Pigott, who collaborated with Malak on one of his many bestselling picture books, Mayor Bob Chiarelli and former mayor Jim Watson, president of the Canadian Tourism Commission. The steps to the church were lined with 32 pots of bright red tulips — the flower which won Malak his fame.

Jean Pigott, who collaborated with Malak on one of his many bestselling picture books, was among the high-profile citizens in attendance, including Ottawa Mayor Bob Chiarelli and former mayor Jim Watson, president of the Canadian Tourism Commission.

The entire staff of the Canadian Tulip Festival — an event Malak spawned in 1951 — attended the service wearing the festival's official yellow jackets.

There was a bittersweet convergence of remembering yesterday in Ottawa: Many who attended the morning's Remembrance Day service at the War Memorial — paying respect for the sacrifices and heroics of Canadian soldiers in war — strolled directly south a few blocks to the church on Elgin Street to share in the sorrow and celebration at Malak's funeral.

Describing him as "a renowned citizen of this city and nation," Rector Garth Bulmer praised Malak as a devoted admirer of his wife and business partner Barbara, as a loving father, grandfather and greatgrandfather, and as an artist "capable of seeing beauty, seeing God, and giving that sight to others."

See **MALAK** on page C6

The casket of Malak Karsh being carried from St. John the Evangelist Anglican Church.

Although it was Malak Karsh who became noted for photographing Ottawa's famous tulips, which are a gift each year from the people of the Netherlands in thanks for the city giving refuge to the Dutch royal family during the Second World War, it is the grave of his brother Yousuf in Notre Dame Cemetery that is adorned with a sculptured tulip. Both men made Ottawa their adopted home and became world famous for their photography.

Lynn Ball / Ottawa Citizen.

Estrellita Karsh, widow of Yousuf Karsh, leaving the gravesite.

Unknown / Courtesy of the McGarry Family Archives.

Stanfield remembered for decency, integrity

Former Tory leader's funeral took place just steps from the goal that eluded him: 24 Sussex Drive. Sean Gordon reports.

FRED CHARTRAND, THE CANADIAN PRESS

The family and close friends of Robert Stanfield gathered to bid farewell yesterday from the steps of a stone church just two blocks away from 24 Sussex Drive, an address the late Conservative leader strove for but never managed to call his own.

Mr. Stanfield, a former Nova Scotia premier who was often called "the best prime minister Canada never had," was remembered in a private 45-minute service at St. Bartholomew's Anglican Church.

The century-old church sits across the street from the grounds of Rideau Hall, the Governor General's official residence.

Mr. Stanfield's wife, children and grand-children huddled alongside friends like his former chief-of-staff, Senator Lowell Murray, and watched silently as a hearse carrying the 89-year-old Mr. Stanfield's coffin drove slowly into the distance.

His remains were then transported to his native Nova Scotia. He is to be buried today in a Halifax cemetery.

The mourners included Gov. Gen. Adrienne Clarkson, former prime ministers Kim Campbell and Joe Clark, who worked as an aide to Mr. Stanfield in the 1970s, Tory caucus leader Peter MacKay, Quebec Premier Jean Charest and Nova Scotia Premier John Hamm.

"It was a nostalgic, kind of sombre mood," said Mr. Murray, who delivered the eulogy.

Prime Minister Paul Martin, whose father had a long friendship with Mr. Stanfield, also attended the ceremony and recalled a principled man who was known above all for his integrity and selfless dedication to public service.

"There's no doubt he had a tremendous sense, not only of Nova Scotia, but of Atlantic Canada and of the whole country. He also had a tremendous sense of what really a political leader should be all about," said Mr. Martin, who praised Mr. Stanfield's "sense of decency, his integrity, his character, and his deep love of the country."

Robert Lorne Stanfield was born in 1914 in Truro, N.S., scion of a family that made its fortune in the undergarment industry.

He entered politics in the 1930s after graduating from Harvard Law School. The federal Tories turned to Mr. Stanfield, then premier of Nova Scotia, in the late 1960s as their answer to new Liberal leader Pierre Trudeau.

When Trudeaumania captivated the country in 1968, it swept the Tories' election chances away with it.

In 1972, Mr. Stanfield came within two seats — and a few hundred votes — of becoming prime minister. He would step down four years later after Mr. Trudeau beat him a third time.

WAYNE CUDDINGTON, THE OTTAWA CITIZEN

WAYNE CUDDINGTON, THE OTTAWA CITIZEN

Robert Stanfield's funeral was a simple and elegant affair at St. Bartholomew's Church near Rideau Hall. Among those in attendance were Prime Minister Paul Martin, top left, shown embracing Mr. Stanfield's widow, Anne. At left, Mrs. Stanfield walks with her sons Bill Austin, left, and Laurie Austin.

Robert Stanfield of Nova Scotia has been described as the best prime minister we never had. In the 1972 general election, this quiet, thoughtful man came within a few seats of defeating Pierre Trudeau. Patrick McGarry, following the casket with Mrs. Stanfield and family, directed the funeral at Ottawa's St. Bartholomew's Anglican Church.

THE OTTAWA CITIZEN   SUNDAY, MARCH 28, 2004 **A5**

CANADA

TOM HANSON, THE CANADIAN PRESS

WAYNE CUDDINGTON, THE OTTAWA CITIZEN   WAYNE CUDDINGTON, THE OTTAWA CITIZEN

Far left, the pews were crowded with Liberals and senior civil servants for the funeral of Mitchell Sharp yesterday, who was remembered for a long life dedicated to public service. Clockwise from top: Paul Martin chats with Supreme Court Chief Justice Beverley McLachlin as Jean Chrétien looks on in the background, the two men conspicuously ignoring each other the whole day; former VIA Rail chairman Jean Pelletier was among the notable guests; Jeanne d'Arc Sharp attended with family; and newlyweds Pinchas Zuckerman and Amanda Forsyth were part of an NAC quintet that performed at the service.

JIM YOUNG, THE CANADIAN PRESS   WAYNE CUDDINGTON, THE OTTAWA CITIZEN

Sharp: 'Great example of public service to the end of his life'

Continued from PAGE A1

The personal feud between Mr. Chrétien and the man who ousted him as prime minister has simmered for years and only intensified with recent revelations of the sponsorship scandal plaguing the government.

The pews were crowded with Liberals and senior civil servants, including former VIA Rail chairman Jean Pelletier, appointed by Mr. Chrétien and fired by Mr. Martin in the wake of the sponsorship scandal.

Many notable politicians did not attend, including Conservative leader Stephen Harper and former prime minister Joe Clark.

Mr. Sharp served as a mentor to Mr. Chrétien during his 40-year parliamentary career. Delivering the main eulogy yesterday, Mr. Chrétien recalled arriving in Ottawa and "not having much knowledge of the country outside of Quebec, I turned to this man."

He described Mr. Sharp as one of Canada's great bureaucrats alongside men such as Lester Pearson and Gordon Robertson; a man with "a very balanced view of things, never going to the extremes ... an internationalist who expected that Canada should play a role in all international forums," and a man who understood "the real workings of government, its powers and its limits ... an optimist by nature."

He described hosting a 90th birthday dinner for Mr. Sharp at 24 Sussex Drive and thanking him for everything he had done over the years. When Mr. Sharp stood up, he thanked everyone and then stressed that he was there not to talk about the past, "I'm here to talk about my future."

Mr. Chrétien said Mr. Sharp was a "great example of public service until the end of his life," and had served as a $1-a-year adviser for the past 10 years. The only time he complained, Mr Chrétien joked, was when the dollar threatened to drop below 60 cents U.S. "and he was worried about feeding his family."

Mr. Chrétien noted that Mr. Sharp had served his "beloved Canada" and four prime ministers before him: Mackenzie King, Louis St. Laurent, Lester Pearson and Pierre Trudeau.

"All my life I turned to him in difficult circumstances," Mr. Chrétien said.

Longtime senior civil servant and diplomat Jack "Jake" Warren recalled the many highlights of Mr. Sharp's six-decade-long career and described him as "a very special Canadian — what splendid images of public service his name evokes. ... His was a life well and fully lived."

It was writer and educator David Leighton who talked of Mr. Sharp's "parallel love affair with music" after a quintet of the National Arts Centre Orchestra — Pinchas Zuckerman and Walter Prystawski, violin; Kimball Sykes, clarinet; Jane Logan, viola; and Amanda Forsyth, cello — performed the larghetto from Mozart's *Clarinet Quintet.*

"Somehow in the midst of all his other accomplishments, Mitchell Sharp managed to become a highly skilled pianist," Mr. Leighton said. "He was a great friend and supporter, a kindly grandfather to the arts centre, especially the orchestra."

He recalled last summer when Mr. Sharp was 92 and quite frail, having his electronic piano hauled up to his summer cottage so that three or four times a day he could sit down and play Mozart and Schubert.

"Unofficially, he was minister in charge of the arts centre," he said.

Yesterday's service was conducted by the Very Rev. Shane Parker, Dean of Ottawa and Rector of Christ Church Cathedral and Cathedral Vicar Rev. Canon William Fairlie.

Mr. Sharp's grandchildren Mitchell Sharp and Dana McLean gave poetry readings and pallbearers were Cathy Campbell, Gordon Farquarson, Peter Herrndorf, Jean Pelletier, Bob Pierce, Gordon Robertson, Basil Robinson and Pauline Sabourin.

Mr. Sharp died on March 19. He is survived by his third wife Jeanne d'Arc Sharp, son Noel from a previous marriage, three grandchildren and five great granddaughters.

Cremation followed the service.

Mitchell Sharp, long-time cabinet minister in the governments of Lester B. Pearson and Pierre Trudeau, and, after retirement, personal adviser to Jean Chrétien, for which he was famously paid one dollar a year.

As the House of Commons' longest-serving sergeant-at-arms (1978–2005), Gus Cloutier provided expert advice for many state occasions. Following a private funeral service where many Hill stories were told, a well-attended memorial service was held for Gus on Parliament Hill. Here, he hosts a Christmas lunch on The Hill for his many old friends. 2003.

Courtesy of the Cloutier Family.

Lloyd Francis, former Speaker of the House of Commons, Kiwanian, dedicated father of three, loving grandfather, and, most of all for the McGarrys, friend. An accomplished amateur lapidarist, the McGarry family treasures the several pieces of jewellery he gave them, fashioned from stones he collected and polished himself.

Courtesy of the Francis Family.

Tom Van Dusen, noted journalist and long-time adviser to prime ministers John Diefenbaker and Brian Mulroney. Father of seven, many of his children have carved out distinguished careers of their own in journalism. His wife, Shirley, is a noted author and painter. Tom is standing on Parliament Hill below the statue of John Diefenbaker.

Courtesy of Shirley Van Dusen.

Four killed in townhouse fire tragedy

By Bob Marleau
Citizen staff writer

A 32-year-old woman and her three sons died early today in a fire in an Elmvale Acres townhouse unit they were to leave in a few days.

Dead are Gail St. Jacques and her three sons, Kevin, 7, David, 12, and Steven, 13, of 1995 St. Laurent Blvd.

Leo St. Jacques, 39, was rescued from a second-floor window by firemen. He suffered burns and cuts.

The dead woman's brother, John Ville-neuve, 27, who had been rooming with the family, managed to escape from his basement bedroom in his underclothing.

Both St. Jacques and Villeneuve were admitted to Riverside Hospital for observation and are listed in satisfactory condition.

Neighbors and passersby who attempted to rescue the family from the 1:30 a.m. fire were driven back by the intense heat.

"I ran over and opened the front door but the whole place was on fire," said Nick Waseluk.

Mrs. St. Jacques had started a new job

Thursday to help pay for a condominium the family had purchased Wednesday and were to move into Monday.

"They couldn't buy it earlier because they had no money," said Fred Blundell a neighbor and family friend. "That's why she returned to work."

When firefighters arrived flames had already engulfed most of the row-end unit. The blaze was confined to the St. Jacques home.

Neighbors wept openly as the bodies were removed.

All the bodies were found in the master bedroom, leading firefighters to speculate the family had clustered in the room when they found themselves trapped.

"God, it was impossible to get into the room," said District Fire Chief Aurele Goderre.

Cause of the fire is not known, but investigators believe it started on the ground floor, either in the living room or kitchen.

Jean Racine, a Canadian National Railways constable on his way to work and one

of the first on the scene, said both St. Jacques and his brother-in-law were hysterical after their escape.

"He was crying 'My kids. My Kids. Are any of my kids out. Please go get my kids'."

Racine said when he arrived, about the same time as firefighters, the doorways and windows were "like burners."

"God. It's terrible to see a whole family wiped out," he said.

(Oh my God, page 4)

Ottawa, Friday, February 17, 1978

The Citizen

135th Year
Number 194
60 Pages

Home delivered
85¢ weekly.
15¢ per copy

Valley Edition

ST. JACQUES

Gail, Steven and David and Kevin. Accidentally at home on Friday, February 17, 1978. Gail Villeneuve, beloved wife of Leo St. Jacques (and dear daughter of Paul and Rita St. Jacques) Steven, David and Kevin St. Jacques, beloved sons of Leo and the late Gail St. Jacques. Gail is also survived by several brothers and sisters. Resting at Hulse and Playfair Central Chapel, 315 McLeod St. after 12 noon on Sunday. Funeral from the Church of the Resurrection of Our Lord, Roman Catholic Church, on Monday at 10 30 a.m. Interment Beechwood Cemetery. P5172P

Grim-looking firefighters, ambulance operators remove one of bodies from burned out townhouse

—Citizen photo

Mourners pay last respects at services in cemetery near Rupert

Hundreds mourn 4 dead

By Peter Maser
Citizen staff writer

Thursday was a grey day in the Gatineau Valley.

Though the afternoon sun shone brightly and a warm wind filled the air with the promise of summer, hundreds of residents from Gatineau to Maniwaki were grieving the loss of four of the valley's most stalwart citizens.

Gathered in a tiny cemetery outside the village of Rupert, they had come to pay their last respects to James Moore, 70; his wife, Evelyn, 57; his brother, Everett, 65; and Everett's wife, Katherine, 57.

Their lives came to a tragic end last Sunday night on Highway 105, a short distance from their Wakefield homes.

It was in Wakefield that James, or Jimmy as his friends knew him, Everett and Evelyn were born and raised. Katherine also spent most of her life in Wakefield, though she hailed from Yarm, a town near Shawville, Que.

And it was in this picturesque village on the banks of the Gatineau River that the Moores came to be loved and respected by their colleagues, friends and neighbors.

"Let's just say they were darned good people," said one mourner, who asked he be referred to only as a good friend of the families.

"They were active in just about everything. Church work, Legion work, youth work around Rupert.

"They were known by everyone in this community and even beyond."

Indeed, it would have been diffi-

The Citizen, Ottawa, Friday, June 8, 1979, Page 3

local

Wakefield couples killed, 'pillars of community' gone

In 1979, Sharon McGarry's two uncles and two aunts died in a horrific car accident. Pillars of the communities of Wakefield and Rupert, Quebec, their funerals drew more than 800 to mourn their loss.

Ottawa, June 9, 1980.

Dear Mr. Lloyd,

I feel compelled to let you know how much I have appreciated the efficient manner in which you made the arrangements for the cremation of our dear son's remains. We hear a lot about funeral directors who appear to exploit people's vulnerability in times of sorrow, but your behavior was a model of uprightness, untainted by any trace of commercialism. You couldn't have done more to make things easier for us and for that, on behalf of my wife and our beloved Michael, I thank you very much indeed.

Very truly yours,

(Lee van Goudoever)

In 2005, five members of the Thach family died in a house fire. Brian's wife, Joan Sun McGarry, who was born in China and advises Hulse, Playfair & McGarry on Asian funeral traditions, directed the funeral.

Unknown / Courtesy of the McGarry Family Archives.

Bob and Bonnie Dagenais, highly respected, retired educators, were murdered in their Val-des-Monts cottage in 2002. Here, family members watch as the hearse leaves St. Patrick's Basilica.   *QMI Agency.*

Painting by Jean Dagenais.

Dear Brian

We wanted to extend our best wishes and let you know that you have been in our thoughts and our prayers.

We pray for your health and well being.

André & Jean Dagenais

In 2004, Bob Dagenais' brother and sister in-law, André and Jean Dagenais, encouraged Brian, who was facing cancer surgery. Funeral directors are so grateful for cards of thanks and enduring relationships with families they have served.

CANADIAN FORCES

Prime Minister Jean Chrétien, his wife, Aline, Toronto funeral director Allan Cole, and Brian arriving at Juno Beach, France, to participate in the opening of the Juno Centre and to assist with the burial of three unknown soldiers at Passchendaele, June 2003. Leading the mission was CWO Paul "Smokey" Leblanc, who became a fun friend of Allan's and Brian's.

Unknown / Courtesy of the McGarry Family Archives.

 Public Works and
Government Services
Canada

Travaux publics et
Services gouvernementaux
Canada

Ceremonial & Protocol Services
Government Conference Centre
2 Rideau Street, Room 301
Ottawa, Ontario
K1N 8X5

7 July 2000

Brian McGarry and Tom Flood
Hulse, Playfair & McGarry Inc.
315 McLeod Street,
Ottawa, Ontario
K2P 1A2

Brian and Tom

Dear Mr. ~~McGarry and Mr Flood~~:

I am just now getting caught up on my correspondence after a busy May and June and I want to thank you both for your letter and photos of the Tomb of the Unknown Soldier.

I have been extremely fortunate to have been able to participate in this wonderful project which, as you say, is a lasting reminder of our country's commitment and sacrifice to the cause of peace and freedom. I have also been fortunate to have been able to turn to you for advice and assistance not only during the planning for the Tomb of the Unknown Soldier but over the past fifteen years when we have participated together in a number of state funerals of distinguished Canadians.

I have been continuously impressed with the integrity, sympathy and knowledge which Hulse, Plairfair and McGarry display during these occasions. The assistance which I received from you during the Tomb planning phase was typical of your commitment, for even though you were to receive no official recognition for your support, you unfailingly provided me with the advice and resources for which I am most grateful.

I hope that these certificates will serve to remind you that your service to Canadians is appreciated.

Gerry Wharton
Manager
Ceremonial & Protocol Services
Tel 613-990- 6769, FAX 613-991-2292
e-mail whartong@pwgsc.gc.ca

Canadä

CERTIFICATE
OF
APPRECIATION

The Royal Canadian Legion
acknowledges with sincere appreciation the
dedication and commitment of

Brian McGarry

in bringing home our Unknown Soldier
and laying him to rest in the

**TOMB OF THE
UNKNOWN SOLDIER**

28 MAY 2000

DUANE DALY
DOMINION SECRETARY
PROJECT CHAIRMAN

BILL BARCLAY
DOMINION PRESIDENT

One unknown soldier from Vimy Ridge, France,
was returned to Ottawa for interment at the
Tomb of the Unknown Soldier.
Courtesy of the McGarry Family Archives.

At the Tomb of the Unknown Soldier beside the War Memorial in Ottawa are Gerry Wharton, Manager of Ceremonial and Protocol Services; Canadian sculptor Mary-Ann Liu; and Tom Flood and Brian McGarry of McGarry Family Chapels. Mary-Ann sculpted the cover of the tomb.

Unknown / Courtesy of the McGarry Family Archives.

The Royal Regiment of Canada and the Queen's Own Rifles of Canada carry the casket of the remains of an unknown soldier of the Great War to his final resting place at the Passchendaele New British Cemetery on June 9, 2003. *Courtesy of the Department of National Defence / WO Jean Blouin.*

Chief of the Defence Staff · Chef d'état-major de la Défense

National Defence
Headquarters
Ottawa, Ontario
K1A 0K2

Quartier général de
la Défense nationale
Ottawa (Ontario)
K1A 0K2

20   December 2005

Mr. Brian McGarry
McGarry Family Chapels
Hulse, Playfair and McGarry
315 McLeod Street
Ottawa, Ontario
K2P 1A2

Dear Mr McGarry,

I would like to thank you for your contribution to the planning and conduct of the lying-in-state ceremonies in Ottawa, ON and Vancouver, BC for Sergeant Smokey Smith, Canada's last surviving recipient of the Victoria Cross.

The ceremonies for Sergeant Smith received the attention of the entire nation, resulting in a poignant farewell to a true Canadian hero, and serving as a reminder to us all of the important sacrifices made by those gone before him, and those who will come after him. It was a clear message to that great generation of Canadians that all they did is remembered and much appreciated, and a sign to serving members that their risky work is important to the nation.

The outstanding support you provided upon arrivals of the remains at the Canada Reception Center, during the ceremony and with the transportation of the family was instrumental to the overall success of this event. Your assistance enabled Canada to honour Sergeant Smith, and all our veterans, with a tribute characterized by grace, honour and dignity.

On behalf of all the men and women of the Canadian Forces, I wish to express my gratitude for the professionalism and dedication you displayed in your efforts to ensure the success of these events. Your contribution brought great credit to you, your company, and Canada.

Thank you,

R.J. Hillier
General

National   Défense
Defence   nationale

Canada

General Rick Hillier, Chief of Defence Staff of the Canadian Forces, took time to express his appreciation for the McGarry Family Chapel's role in the funeral ceremonies for Sergeant Ernest Smokey Smith, Canada's last surviving recipient of the Victoria Cross. The medal is awarded for gallantry in the face of the enemy and was presented to Smith after he single-handedly held off German tanks and soldiers near the small, northern Italian town of San Giorgio Di Cesena in 1944. Prime Minister Paul Martin offered a state funeral to Sergeant Smith's family, and they accepted. The lying-in-state occurred in the foyer of the House of Commons; Sergeant Smith was only the ninth person to be accorded this honour. Funeral director Thomas Crean, of Vancouver, arranged for the cremation of Sergeant Smith and burial at sea, following the state funeral. 2005.
Courtesy of the McGarry Family Archives.

Sergeant Smith's casket arrives in the Centre Block, Parliament Hill. The casket was made of Victoriaville Maple, a wood often used for veterans and soldiers. 2005.

Allan Cole.

Passing through the Rotunda of the Centre Block. Brian and Sharon McGarry are pictured behind the medal bearer. The person who took this photo is Allan Cole, the funeral director largely responsible for bringing our fallen Canadian soldiers home from Afghanistan. 2005.

Allan Cole.

Royal Canadian Mounted Police   Gendarmerie royale du Canada

G. Zaccardelli
Commissioner   Le Commissaire

Mr. Brian McGarry
Owner
McGarry Family Chapels

Mrs. Sharon McGarry
Co-Owner, President
McGarry Family Chapels

Mr. Donald Renaud
Manager/Director
McGarry Family Chapels

Dear Sirs and Madam:

As the holidays approach, I am not only reflecting on my immediate family and how invaluable it will be to spend time with them, but as Commissioner of the Royal Canadian Mounted Police (RCMP), I am also thinking of my extended RCMP family.

It is with heartfelt sorrow that I must reflect on the most recent deaths of two of our members, Constables Marc Bourdages and Robin Cameron. The tragic loss we suffered this past summer in Saskatchewan, and the loss last year of four of our members in the Mayerthorpe tragedy, truly affected us as an organization.

However, through our sorrow, we have been most fortuitous to have McGarry Family Chapels helping us along the way. You have provided us with incredible compassion, support and leadership in these last two years, and have helped us to properly memorialize these fallen members. You have been there for us within a moment's call, at no cost, and we treasure your precious support.

I believe that it is an opportune time of year to celebrate the special partnership that exists between the RCMP and McGarry Family Chapels. In this regard, I understand that an informal get-together is being arranged to personally thank you for your most gracious and generous support. Superintendent Greg Peters, Director, Strategic Partnerships and Heritage Branch, will be contacting you in the New Year to make mutually convenient arrangements.

Please accept my most sincere appreciation for your help these past years. Together, we will continue to remember our fallen members.

Sincerely,

G. Zaccardelli
G. Zaccardelli

1200 Vanier Parkway   1200, promenade Vanier
Ottawa, Ontario   Ottawa (Ontario)
K1A 0R2   K1A 0R2

Courtesy of the McGarry Family Archives.

Constable Anthony Gordon.

Constable Lionide Johnston.

Constable Brock Myrol.

Constable Peter Schiemann.

Const. Annie Gagnon carries a portrait of Const. Anthony Gordon, one of four slain RCMP officers, during a memorial service at Christ Church Cathedral in Ottawa yesterday.

WAYNE CUDDINGTON, THE OTTAWA CITIZEN

'All of us knew them as our brothers'

Hundreds come from far and wide for memorial service in Ottawa

BY PAULA MCCOOEY

Hundreds of members of the law enforcement community showed strength and solidarity yesterday at an Ottawa memorial service to honour four fallen RCMP officers.

Six religious leaders led the service at Christ Church Cathedral on Sparks Street. A live feed was broadcast at the adjacent church, St. Peter's Lutheran Church, to accommodate those who could not find space at Christ Church.

Rabbi Arnie Fine asked that the 500-plus audience — including officers with the U.S. Border Patrol and others who travelled to Ottawa from Eastern Canada — to pray for the families, friends and colleagues of the young constables Peter Schiemann, 25, Lionide Johnston, 32, Anthony Gordon, 28, and Brock Myrol, 29.

"All of us across this country knew them (the four officers) as our brothers," said Rabbi Fine.

"We pray that you send your grace and love to their parents, spouses, and children as they wrestle with the huge gaps in their lives, their emotions and dreams which are now shattered. And let us all reflect on the enormity of their sacrifice, their devotion to the welfare of the communities they served and may they rest in heaven."

Sikh Baldev Singh Vij also asked his audience to pray for the victims' families and, somehow, find strength amidst their grief.

"We have lost dear friends in the line of duty," said Mr. Vij. "God knows why these things happen and all we can do is pray to him and ask to give strength to family and friends."

Guest were later invited to sign a book of condolences at the Musical Ride visitor centre located at the RCMP stables on St. Laurent Boulevard to express their sympathies.

Greg Meredith and Cheryl Fraser represented Correctional Services Canada at yesterday's ceremony.

As an organization that works closely with police across Canada, they said their presence was important.

"We are very much tied into the public safety system of the country," said Ms. Fraser, as she left the downtown church. "And it's important, being part of the same justice system, that we very much recognize each other's work in the community and each other's contribution."

Mr. Meredith said the death of the officers "hits home".

"Our staff feel very, very close to the police when they go through a tragedy like this. You are dealing with offenders, either in terms of bringing them in, or trying to get them back into the community. So when a tragedy like this happens, I think the (law enforcement) community really comes in as a family."

Eighteen-year-old Amy Mole, a student at Algonquin College's police foundations program, volunteered for yesterday's memorial. She said the officers' deaths will not deter her from following her dream of becoming a police officer.

"It (the killings) pushes me harder toward what I want to do now," said Ms. Mole. "To help control all these problems, and these people who are causing problems. It makes me feel stronger about trying to get out there and help."

After the commemoration, visitors stayed to watch the live ceremony that transformed Edmonton into the setting for a national day of mourning.

Memorial service held in Ottawa for the four RCMP officers who were slain at Mayerthorpe, Alberta, 2005.

The four RCMP officers slain at
Mayerthorpe, Alberta, March 3, 2005.
Courtesy of the Royal Canadian Mounted Police.

Courtesy of the McGarry Family Archives.

A new protocol was developed for folding the Canadian flag at the gravesites during military, RCMP, and state funerals. CWO Paul "Smokey" Leblanc (fourth from left) was involved in developing the procedure.

Courtesy of the McGarry Family Archives.

A proud day for the McGarry-Schwerdfeger families, as Ryan Schwerdfeger graduates from the RCMP Academy, Depot Division, in Regina, 2008.

Courtesy of the Royal Canadian Mounted Police.

Governor General Ed Schreyer welcomes Kiwanis university members, known as Circle K, to Government House. The young people gave the governor general a gold night clock, which somehow got misplaced. Mr. Schreyer called Brian at home to explain the situation and asked if a replacement could be arranged. At first Brian thought a Kiwanian was pulling his leg, but, fortunately, before embarrassing himself, he realized that it really was the governor general on the other end of the line. 1980.

Tsin Van / Courtesy of the McGarry Family Archives.

In 1990, David Peterson, Premier of Ontario, called an early, snap election before his term was complete. Although Brian was asked to run for the Liberals in Ottawa Centre, he declined, knowing that this riding was nearly impossible for a businessperson to win. It proved a smart move, as Ontarians made the radical move of replacing Peterson's Liberals with the New Democratic Party under the leadership of Bob Rae. Evelyn Gigantes won the riding for the NDP.

Courtesy of the Office of the Premier of Ontario.

Brian with best wishes Brian Mulroney

There are those who disagree with the suggestion that Brian Mulroney was one of Canada's great prime ministers. Free trade with the United States and replacing the complicated federal sales tax with the GST are just two of the policies his government introduced that set the foundation for Canada's recovery from a severe economic downturn in the early 1990s. He was, and continues to be, highly regarded on the international stage. This photo was taken in 1991, at a reception for Russian president Boris Yeltsin at the National Art Gallery of Canada.

Courtesy of the Prime Minister's Office.

CANADA

PRIME MINISTER · PREMIÈRE MINISTRE

November 4, 1992

Dear Brian,

I want to thank you for your kind note of October 30 and for the important, responsible contribution you have made to the cause of greater national unity.

Despite our disappointment of the 26th, we shall soldier on; there is much more to do, and it is as important. Your continuing support is very important to me.

With my best personal regards,

Yours sincerely,

Mr. Brian McGarry,
President,
Hulse, Playfair & McGarry,
315 McLeod Street,
Ottawa, Ontario.
K2P 1A2

Disappointment concerning the defeat of the Charlottetown Accord, a set of amendments meant to persuade the government of Quebec to endorse the Canadian Constitution of 1982 and increase support in Quebec for remaining within Canada. Brian, like many Canadians, worked hard during the national referendum held that fall of 1992 to keep Canada together.

Courtesy of the McGarry Family Archives.

Canada's constitutional crisis continued through the decade, and in October 1995, Quebec held a referendum on sovereignty. One of the most stirring moments of the referendum campaign was the rally in Montreal, three days before the vote, when approximately 100,000 Canadians from in and outside Quebec came to celebrate a united Canada and plead with Quebecers to vote "No." Held at Place du Canada, it was Canada's biggest political rally.

In 1996, former Quebec premier Daniel Johnson came to Ottawa to speak to Dialogue Canada about the impact of the referendum. Here, he was presented with a copy of the famous photograph from the rally by Brian McGarry and Paul Salvatore, co-founders of the Ottawa chapter of Dialogue Canada.

Barry Schwerdfeger.

Governance and Leadership

Another great prime minister, Jean Chrétien. To his right, former MP Mac Harb; to his left, former Speaker of the House of Commons, Lloyd Francis, both representing ridings in Ottawa. This photo was taken not long before Mr. Chrétien retired as Leader of the Liberal Party in 2003.

Courtesy of the Prime Minister's Office.

CANADA

LEADER OF THE OPPOSITION — CHEF DE L'OPPOSITION

BRIAN WILLIAM MCGARRY

Tonight you are honouring a very special Canadian. At a time when Canada needs all the insight and good will of its citizens - Brian McGarry stands out as a symbol of what is best in Canadians.

I am very pleased to join with the B'nai B'rith Ottawa Lodge #885 in paying tribute to Brian, whom you have chosen as the 1991 Ottawa Citizen of the Year.

Brian will be receiving many well-deserved accolades tonight. His accomplishments are many. I can mention only a few: his efforts to improve legislation affecting the public and his profession, his work with Kiwanis International, and his service as a Trustee of the Ottawa Board of Education.

For the past thirty years, he has devoted his energies to finding new bonds and new endeavours that reflect our collective Canadian values - the values of fairness, sharing, tolerance and compassion. Brian is an exceptional leader, and has used his talents to benefit the people of the National Capital Region and the greater community.

My very best wishes to you and your family, Brian for an evening of warmth and friendship, and for continued success in the years to come.

Jean Chrétien

OTTAWA
June 9, 1992

CANADA

PRIME MINISTER · PREMIÈRE MINISTRE

November 3, 1993

Dear Brian,

I want to join with your family, friends, and colleagues in congratulating you on being named Business Person of the Year for 1993 by the Ottawa-Carleton Board of Trade.

Your commitment to the development of an economic strategy for the National Capital Region and the responsible positions you have adopted on larger issues have shown a deep commitment to community and country. Publicly and privately your entire family has worked tirelessly for the betterment of us all.

I wish you, Sharon, Brett and Erin health, happiness and every success in the years to come.

With my best regards,

Yours sincerely,

Mr. Brian McGarry

Kim Campbell never really had a chance to show her strengths during her short tenure as prime minister in 1993. She had a good grasp of Canadian values, once describing us as decaffeinated Americans. This was probably a compliment to both nations. From left to right: Gary Boxma, an accomplished Kiwanian as well as a dear friend; Prime Minister Kim Campbell; Brian McGarry; and Shirley Westeinde, a prominent member of the Ottawa business community. 1993.
Barry Schwerdfeger.

Governance and Leadership

 From left to right: Jean Charest, Leader of the Progressive Conservative Party; Lloyd Francis, Speaker of the House of Commons; and Brian McGarry. The note on the photo by Jean Charest reads: "Brian, why does Mr. Francis look to be so worried? Probably something you said!" 1994.

Barry Schwerdfeger.

From left to right: Jean Charest; Sharon McGarry; Brian's brother-in-law, Barry Schwerdfeger; and Jean Charest's wife, Michèle Dionne. 1994.

Office of the Leader of the Official Opposition.

Would you believe that a fifteen-year anniversary for the state funeral of John Diefenbaker was held in the Centre Block on Parliament Hill? Rare is a funeral anniversary ever celebrated, but Dief's funeral was special, meriting a film by the National Film Board of Canada.

Diefenbaker's funeral was one of the most complicated in Canada's history, involving transport by train and plane, and the disinterment of his wife's remains from Beechwood Cemetery in Ottawa, which were reburied alongside him on the grounds of the University of Saskatchewan, Saskatoon. Hundreds of friends and funeral organizers came from across Canada for the 1994 reunion. From left to right: Brian McGarry; Sharon McGarry, President of Hulse, Playfair & McGarry; former prime minister Joe Clark; and Chief of Protocol, Graham Glockling.
Barry Schwerdfeger.

Alberta premier Ralph Klein with Sharon McGarry and Brian McGarry, 1997. Premier Klein was speaking in Ottawa to the local chapter of Dialogue Canada. Midway through Mr. Klein's presentation, a heckler interrupted. When she had finished her scolding, Mr. Klein calmly said, "You know, miss? You have made my day. Here, in Ottawa, I thought there might be a day in my life without heckling. But, no, you have proved me wrong. Now I still have a 100 percent unbroken record of a heckler or three, every day of my life! "

Later, Brian made his way, along with Paul Salvatore, co-founder of Dialogue Canada, and others to McGill University, where Mr. Klein and noted Canadian historian Desmond Morton were scheduled to take part in a panel discussion. Mr. Klein was late to arrive. Asked why he was late, he replied, "I spent a couple of hours in Montreal coffee shops listening to real Canadians." That's why he remained premier for fourteen years.

Barry Schwerdfeger.

Governance and Leadership

During a seniors' reception held for the Queen and the Duke of Edinburgh, Prince Philip asked Brian and Sharon's young daughter, Erin, "What are you doing at a party for old fogeys?" Erin, tight-lipped, thought it best not to attempt a reply, so simply said, "Good morning." Left to right: Jackie Holzman, Mayor of Ottawa; Elizabeth II; Sharon McGarry; Brian McGarry; and Erin McGarry. June 1997.

Tsin Van / Courtesy of the McGarry Family Archives.

Ottawa Centre MP Mac Harb, Prime Minister Jean Chrétien, and Brian chat in the Prime Minister's Office about the Liberals' recent win in the 2000 federal election. Mr. Chrétien, who would retire before the next election, already knew of Brian's acquaintance with Stephen and Laureen Harper; Brian believed that the Liberal Party would have a tough time after Mr. Chrétien left. Mr. Chrétien and Mac chided Brian, saying, "Beware of those divided Conservatives." They had great fun, but sure enough, Stephen Harper was able to achieve the near impossible and united the Conservatives, garnering enough support so as to form the government in 2006. Many Liberals, possibly including the man himself, may have underestimated Jean Chrétien's connection with ordinary Canadians.

Jean-Marc Carisse.

Governance and Leadership

Former prime minister John Turner chatting with Brian and Sharon McGarry. After retiring from politics, Mr. Turner joined the board of directors of The Loewen Group, one of the largest funeral conglomerates in North America. One of his most difficult days occurred when he had to ask Ray Loewen to step down as head of the company Ray had founded. Ray and his wife, Anne, were principled people, but ran into trouble in the late 1990s with the State of Mississippi, which resulted in a $170 million lawsuit settlement.

Courtesy of the Ottawa City Hall.

At a garden party at 24 Sussex with Prime Minister Paul Martin, 2005. Charles Hulse was a friend of Paul Martin Sr.

Courtesy of the Prime Minister's Office.

Governance and Leadership

Joan Sun McGarry looks on in quiet amusement during a conversation between the two Brians about Brian McGarry's candidacy for the federal election in Ottawa Centre. 2008.

Jean-Marc Carisse.

The McGarrys are co-founders of the Ottawa Chapter of Dialogue Canada, an organization that provides Canadians with opportunities to know each other better and to acknowledge their differences, to share their respective concerns, and to exchange their vision of the country's future. 1993. *QMI Agency.*

All staff members of Hulse, Playfair & McGarry and its sister company, McGarry Family Chapels / Cremation Centres, are expected to give back to the community. Here, Brian McGarry is being sworn in as a councillor for the Regional Municipality of Ottawa–Carleton; he had previously served nine years on the Ottawa Board of Education. 1994.

Courtesy of the Regional Government of Ottawa–Carleton.

The McGarrys' flagship, Central Chapel, has literally served everyone, from paupers to prime ministers. Here, Ottawa mayor Jim Watson, second from the left, congratulates senior vice-president Tom Flood (left), Brian McGarry, and his brother-in-law, Barry Schwerdfeger, on the addition to their Central Chapel, which preserved the heritage appearance of this building. 1999.

Courtesy of the City of Ottawa.

Member of the Community

Approximately fifty of our staff welcomed Mayor Jim Watson to the opening of our addition to the Central Chapel, 1999. While a number of our staff over the years have moved on to bigger and better things, many have become long-time loyal soldiers, and some even employee-partners, part of our tradition as a family-owned and operated funeral service to the Ottawa community.

Courtesy of the City of Ottawa.

Hockey is in our genes, some more blessed than others! Here, Patrick McGarry plays goal with the Fort Worth Fire (Texas) of the Central Hockey League in the mid-1990s. Although he was drafted by the Toronto Maple Leafs, Patrick did not play in the NHL, but ended his career in 1995 with the Kansas City Blades of the IHL. He subsequently joined the McGarry clan in funeral/cremation services and has since risen to the position of partner and chief operating officer.

Courtesy of the Fort Worth Fire.

Patrick McGarry plays goal with the Fort Worth Fire.

Courtesy of the Fort Worth Fire.

A young Brett McGarry meets The Great One, Wayne Gretzky, 1992. Today, Brett practises law in Ottawa, as does his wife, Anne Tardif. They have two young children, a son, Bobby and a daughter, Sacha. Brett's sister, Erin, is studying to become a veterinarian.

Courtesy of the McGarry Family Archives.

A family of goalies. Here, Brett follows in the footsteps of his cousins Patrick and Robin, as he plays between the pipes for his high school, Glebe Collegiate Institute. 1997.

Unknown / Courtesy of the McGarry Family Archives.

BUSINESS

Editor: Robert Bostelaar, 613-726-5819 • business@thecitizen.canwest.com

JULIE OLIVER, THE OTTAWA CITIZEN

Brett McGarry, left, who joined his father, Brian McGarry, one of the Senators' founders, in Tampa for the celebrations when the Senators were awarded a franchise in 1990, is getting married next Saturday, the same day his beloved team could be playing in Game 6 of the Stanley Cup final. Father Brian intends to offer hurried congratulations, then hustle to Scotiabank Place to watch the game from his corporate suite.

Senators' suite spot

The battle for seats in Scotiabank Place's corporate boxes is almost as intense as the action on the ice, writes **BERT HILL**.

Psst, got a ticket? Brett McGarry is getting married the same day that the Ottawa Senators could be playing game six of the Stanley Cup finals.

What's that got to do with the Senators? Well, his father Brian McGarry, the funeral home owner and former school board trustee, has six seats in Suite 115B, one of the sweetest in the rink, between centre ice and the blue line.

"I got an offer of $1,000 per ticket," said the older Mr. McGarry. "I don't know how they found out but they just assumed that the McGarry family won't be using the seats that night."

Wrong.

Mr. McGarry has promised to keep his speech short.

"The wedding is at 5:15 which should give us time to get to the game. We might not be there for the first face-off, but we hope the Senators raise the cup that night."

The demand for Ottawa Senators tickets is going through the roof as the team plays in its first Stanley Cup final and, despite steep hikes in prices, the organization can't keep up.

Nowhere is the pressure more intense than in the 150 corporate suites at the club and gallery levels.

Mr. McGarry originally got his right to the box as one of the early investors in the franchise. Bradley, then 10, went to Tampa with his father for the celebration when the Senators won its NHL franchise.

Mr. McGarry kept the suite through thick and thin, starting at about $20,000 per season when the Senators played in the Civic Centre. Today, the box costs $160,000 per year and Mr. McGarry splits the seats with other companies to spread out the cost.

There was a time when the Senators had trouble selling suites and the higher-priced tickets in the lower bowl closest to the ice.

Those days are long gone. In fact, said Senators and Scotiabank Place chief operating officer Cyril Leeder, the demand can lead to problems.

"The local executives have had the use of the company suite all year. But now the CEO is coming into town and wants the suite for the finals (so the local executives look for one for themselves. There is no way to meet the demand."

For the average fan who might be able to afford to see one live game a year, this might seem to be a pleasant problem. But it can get intense, particularly when family members, customers and employees get into the act.

Roger Greenberg, the chief executive at Minto Developments, said his sister and a son will be going to tonight's game.

See SUITES on PAGE C4

The McGarry family helps to bring back the Ottawa Senators, 1991.

Few believed that the Ottawa Senators would ever be revived, as depicted in this cartoon by Alan King of Mayor Jim Durrell and Brian McGarry. We did, along with friend Rod Bryden, a brilliant businessperson who built the team's new home, today known as Scotiabank Place; Bruce Firestone and family; Cyril Leeder; and sixty-seven limited partners. April 1991. *Alan King.*

QMI Agency.

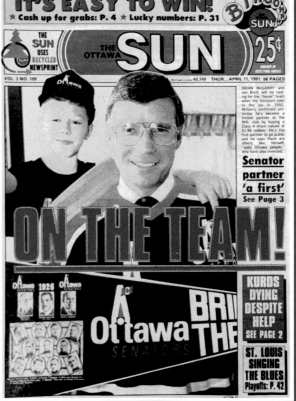

April 1991.

QMI Agency.

Member of the Community

Dad and daughter Erin getting ready for the NHL playoffs at the Corel Centre (now Scotiabank Place). 1998.

Joan Sun McGarry.

Son Brett and nephew Tyler Schwerdfeger enjoying the winter fire at Sharon and Brian's country home in Wakefield, Quebec, 1983.

Barry Schwerdfeger.

Cousins Brett and Tyler at the Corel Centre (Scotiabank Place), 1996. At the time, Brett played goal for the West Ottawa Knights under the coaching tutelage of Glen Richardson, father of long-time NHL defenceman and fellow Knights alumni, Luke Richardson.

Barry Schwerdfeger.

Prime Minister Stephen Harper, Brian's daughter Sheetza McGarry, and Brian attend a Sens game, 2006. Mr. Harper is a knowledgeable hockey fan and has written a book on the sport, scheduled for release in 2012. Where does he find the time?

Courtesy of the Prime Minister's Office.

Two beautiful daughters, Erin and Sheetza McGarry. The McGarrys are attending Erin's high school graduation party at the National Art Gallery, Ottawa, 2006.

Joan Sun McGarry.

Brian McGarry with his daughter Erin.

Helene Anne Fortin.

Sharon and Brian's son, Brett, and his wife, Anne Tardif. Brett and Anne both graduated in law from Dalhousie University and now practise in Ottawa. They are parents to Sharon and Brian's two beautiful grandchildren, Bobby and Sacha.
Joan Sun McGarry.

Sharon and Brian's two beautiful grandchildren, Bobby and Sacha. *Courtesy of Brett McGarry and Anne Tardif.*

Erin and Sheetza McGarry.
Helene Anne Fortin.

Member of the Community

Patrick McGarry, Sharon McGarry, and Brian McGarry accept the award presented by Gisèle Lalonde to Brian McGarry and the McGarry Chapels for contributing to the Montfort Hospital fundraising campaign.

Pascal Boraschi / Courtesy of the Montfort Hospital Foundation.

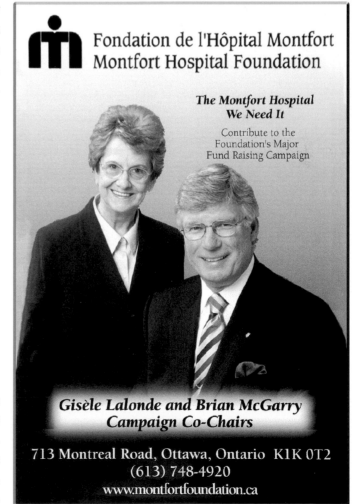

Both the francophone and anglophone communities of Ottawa came together to raise funds for the rejuvenated Montfort Hospital. Here, Gisèle Lalonde and Brian create a television advertisement in support of the campaign.

Courtesy of the Montfort Hospital Foundation.

A new era. The McGarrys opened their first crematorium in Wakefield, Quebec, in 1998. We continue to look for new ways that provide more green alternatives to burial in expensive cemetery grounds. One alternative is resomation, a water/alkali-based method that is both dignified and respectful. We continue to respect faith-based and community-based cemeteries, but are fiercely opposed to corporate cemeteries, where the emphasis is on sales, rather than families.

As this book goes to press, the McGarrys are pleased to announce the purchase of the Cummings Funeral Home in North Gower and the Grant Brown Funeral Homes in Kemptville and Spencerville. With these purchases, Brown & Cummings Chapels will remain family-owned.

Courtesy of the McGarry Family Archives.

Brian McGarry and his family hosted a public unveiling of their new funeral home and crematorium in Wakefield. Among the guests were family friends ABC news anchor Peter Jennings and former governor general of Canada Raymon Hnatyshyn and his wife, Gerda.

Peter Jennings shared his books with the McGarrys and even wrote poetry for Brian's B'nai Brith Citizen of the Year Award banquet in 1992. Sadly, Peter was taken from us all too soon in 2005.

Courtesy of the
McGarry Family Archives

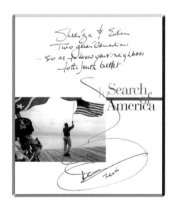

Clockwise from the top right is Peter Jennings, his wife, ABC producer Kayce Freed, sister Sarah Jennings, daughter Liz and son Chris. Below, Peter Jennings, Kayce Freed, Brian, Erin, and Sharon McGarry; and Gerda and Ray Hnatyshyn.

Yvonne Berg / Ottawa Citizen.

B'nai Brith, Ottawa Lodge No. 885, presented Brian McGarry with the 1992 Citizen of the Year award at a gala dinner attended by over 600 people. Here Brian McGarry addresses the gathering with Rabbi Bulka listening attentively. June 1992.

Andrew Balfour Photography.

PETER JENNINGS

June 9, 1992

Dear Brian,

I am so very sorry that I am not there in person, though
it probably suits the occasion to say that I am there "in spirit."

It seems only suitable that I should participate in honoring you.

Thirty years ago when I, as a young man,
intoned on your earliest television commercials

"those you _care_, use Hulse and Playfair,"

people finally began to pay attention.

In other words, where would you be today?

More recently, now that you have finally become
a respectable member of the community, you were there

to help all the Jennings in that important but sad

moment of passage in a family's life.

Aside from your general efficiency at Mother's funeral,

heaven forbid it should have been otherwise,

I wish I were there tonight to tell you in person

how sensitive you were to the whole occasion.

Thus, I intone, this time without a fee:

"When you choose to marry, ignore McGarry.

For the _final requirement_ do not tarry."

Peter Jennings wrote a poem to Brian,
which was read out on the occasion.

Courtesy of the McGarry Family Archives.

One of the highlights of the evening,
Brett McGarry, then twelve years old, spoke for the
Kids of Canada and received a standing ovation.

B'nai. B'rith — Ottawa Lodge No. 885
Proudly Presents Its 1966
Citation Award Dinner
Honouring
MR. CHARLES H. HULSE
as "Citizen of the Year, 1965"

Jewish Community Centre
MONDAY, MARCH 28, 1966

B'nai Brith, Ottawa Lodge No. 885, presented Charles Hulse
with the Citizen of the Year award in 1965.

Vintage cars belonging to
Charles Hulse and Keith
Playfair. We are donating
the Packards to museums in
Ottawa.

*Courtesy of the McGarry Family
Archives.*

Hulse & Playfair old-timers. Brian worked with the three gentlemen on the right:
Cameron Weagant (twenty-two years), Art Dupuis (twenty-four years), Laird Barclay
(forty-three years). Laird rose to corporate partner and senior vice-president. He missed
only three days of work throughout his entire career.

Courtesy of the Laird Barclay Archives.

At the podium, The Viscount Alexander of Tunis, Governor General of Canada, 1946–52, at the Château Laurier. To his right is Charles Hulse, who at one time was rumoured to be a candidate for the vice-regal position. He would have been excellent. Charlie didn't commit to any political party and enjoyed friendships with those of many political stripes.

Newton Photographers.

Hulse, Playfair & McGarry management team, with Yousuf Karsh's famous photograph
of Winston Churchill overlooking our deliberations. 1990s.

Barry Schwerdfeger.

Courtesy of the McGarry Family Archives.

*Courtesy of the
McGarry Family Archives.*

The funeral home to Ottawa's elite

In its 75-year history,
Hulse, Playfair
& McGarry has
overseen some of the
city's most high-
profile funerals.
Kelly Egan reports.

O ne day in the spring of 1925, Charles H. Hulse, an ambitious casket salesman from Toronto, checked into the Château Laurier on a mission of mercy.

The next morning, the dapper young man took a cab to a brick house at 315 McLeod St. to take the measure of a possible corpse: The Woodburn Funeral Home was on its deathbed and Mr. Hulse's employer, Dominion Manufacturers, was a major creditor.

"Charlie, try to fix things," Mr. Hulse was asked.

In an act of unintended irony, Mr. Hulse came up with a plan to resuscitate his first Ottawa client, not bury him. At the age of 26, he scoped out the company, then bought it on the installment plan.

In a very tangible way, he had begun to alter the course of Ottawa's history.

Hulse, Playfair & McGarry turns 75 this spring — the exact date is unknown — after something like 64,550 funerals, an awesome mass of humanity, big and small.

Over time, it became the place where Ottawa's elite went to be laid to rest: eight state funerals, three prime ministers, four governors-general, two chief justices, mayors, judges, police chiefs, journalists, bishops, diplomats, businessmen, broadcasters and senators.

There were lions of the right (Tory prime minister John Diefenbaker), the centre (Liberal prime ministers Mackenzie King and Lester Pearson) and the left (NDP leader Tommy Douglas and NDP MP Stanley Knowles). Death being the great equalizer, there were paupers and murder victims, and fatalities by every conceivable means — cars, crossbows, trains and planes, lakes and rivers.

It is remarkable to think all of this began with a man, this Charles H. Hulse, a $25-a-week casket salesman, known to bum cigarettes from gravediggers and who could never officially use his best slogan: No Pulse? Call Hulse.

In a sense, Mr. Hulse, who died in 1987, has never gone away. He just became Brian McGarry, 56, the current chief executive officer of the firm, that now handles 1,500 services a year in five locations.

"We hit it off immediately," Mr. McGarry said last week, of his initial meeting with Mr. Hulse in 1962. "I took to it right away. I tagged along behind Charlie Hulse and he became my mentor."

Mr. Hulse, described as "debonair" in old newspaper reports, retired in 1964, two years after Mr. McGarry joined the firm, and by then he was a fixture in the city. He knew anybody who was anybody and buried many of them.

"Some might say he taught me from the top down," said Mr. McGarry, who gained majority ownership of the firm in 1987 with his first wife Sharon, who remains president.

"He introduced me to a cross-section of society that I would never, ever, have met without knowing Charlie Hulse."

One day, recalled Mr. McGarry, the older man called him over into the apartment that is part of the flagship facility on McLeod Street.

"Gary, come in here," he apparently said, mixing up the young man's name. "I want you to meet someone." And, sure enough, sitting at his kitchen table was John Diefenbaker, prime minister of Canada from 1957 to 1963.

Mr. Hulse was a rare creature. In a profession known for its stiff, reserved manners, he had a large public profile, became political without being partisan, and, without a great formal education, managed to have the ear of Ottawa's upper crust.

The parallels in their careers are uncanny.

Mr. Hulse was a trustee (31 years) and later chair of the school board. So was Mr. McGarry, who also served as a regional councillor. Mr. Hulse was an international-level member of the Kiwanis. So is Mr. McGarry.

Both were noted fund-raisers and A-list members in political circles. Both were named B'nai Brith Citizen of the Year. Both began with little money but became wealthy. (Mr. Hulse, however, was never a member of the Elvis Sighting Society.)

Mr. McGarry, a native of Wakefield, has shrewdly invested in popular causes. He was one of the first local investors in the Ottawa Senators, ran national unity ads during the Charlottetown Accord days of 1992, and has been a mover and shaker at the Ottawa-Carleton Board of Trade.

"It's amazing. I'm sure I've copied it, inadvertently or not," said Mr. McGarry, when asked about the similarities in their lives.

It is a minor miracle that Hulse, Playfair & McGarry is here at all, luck playing such an important role in the early days.

In 1926, Mr. Hulse, in partnership with his brother, Percy, had built the business as best they could but they came to a stark realization. There was only enough income to support one family: Somebody had to go.

In a story Mr. Hulse would repeat often, they decided to flip a coin. Charles stayed and Percy moved on, setting up his own funeral home in St. Catharines.

The coin toss was chancy enough, but nothing compared to luck's twist in 1927.

'I really believe we've become an institution in this city.'

Brian McGarry

Mr. Hulse had decided to buy a brand new ambulance, a rarity then in the city. In preparation for an historic visit by Charles Lindbergh, then a world-famous flyer, a federal official asked Mr. Hulse to be on hand at the airport, mostly for appearances.

Here at the invitation of prime minister Mackenzie King, Mr. Lindbergh set the *Spirit of St. Louis* down at 1:19 p.m. on July 2 at what is now the Ottawa International Airport.

Minutes after Mr. Lindbergh landed, his Curtiss P-1B escort planes sprang into a formation. Thousands were watching.

One of the pilots, Lieut. John (Thad) Johnson, lost control of his aircraft, and bailed out, only a couple of hundred metres from the ground. His parachute never fully deployed and Lieut. Johnson hurtled towards the ground.

Who, but Charlie Hulse, to attend to the scene? The ambulance took the pilot to the hospital, but he did not survive. Prime minister King decided that only a grand funeral would do and turned to Mr. Hulse to handle things.

So began the relationship between Hulse and official Ottawa that endures to this day. Keith Playfair joined the firm in the early 1930's and in 1936 the partners bought their rented McLeod Street building. They added the chapel in 1938, choosing an ecclesiastical design and a stone that would harmonize with the Parliament Buildings.

Mr. McGarry arrived in 1962 at the age of 17, working with both Mr. Hulse and Mr. Playfair, who died in 1973.

The lessons learned from his mentor served Mr. McGarry well in 1997 when the great parliamentarian, Stanley Knowles, died at the age of 88. Protocol dictated he was not entitled to a state funeral. But didn't he deserve something on the Hill, after spending 50 years there?

Mr. McGarry called the office of an old friend, Joyce Fairbairn, a Liberal senator. After a moment or two, he was patched through to Ms. Fairbairn on an airplane, travelling with Prime Minister Jean Chrétien during an election.

He explained the problem. She listened, said she'd check with the Big Guy. A moment later, she was back on the line, offering the entrance to the House of Commons as place for people to pay their respects. Would that do?

So it happened and hundreds of people attended to pay their respects.

"And David Knowles, Mr. Knowles' son, remains a good friend to this day."

Mr. McGarry, who still retains something of the Boy Scout in him, has a stockpile of wonderful anecdotes, like the saga of the dying wishes of Mr. Diefenbaker.

When the Chief died in 1979, he probably had the most elaborate and expensive (roughly $500,000) funeral in Canadian history.

Mr. McGarry said Mr. Diefenbaker's original plan was to be buried in Ottawa's Beechwood Cemetery where his second wife Olive was already buried.

Near the end of his days, he changed his mind, deciding he should be hauled 3,000 kilometres by funeral train to Saskatoon, with stops along the way.

There was one other catch. He wanted Olive brought with him. Mr. McGarry said she had to be disinterred the day before his burial and flown to Saskatoon to meet his remains. Their caskets were lowered side by side.

Mr. Diefenbaker was contrary to the end. Never a fan of the new Canadian flag, he asked that he be draped with the old Red Ensign. Hulse had to find a seamstress to hurriedly stitch one together.

"The train was a marvelous experience," said Mr. McGarry, of the ride west. "It was an experience I'll never forget."

It was amazing, he said, to find hundreds of people waiting in the dark, at unscheduled stops, just for a glimpse of the former Tory Chief going by.

As for the future, Mr. McGarry said he is following another piece of Mr. Hulse's advice: look constantly towards expansion. The company has three suburban properties it intends to develop, the first being in Kanata, which should be open in 2001. New funeral homes in Barrhaven and Orleans are on the drawing board.

Employee ownership has always been an important element in the company's history. Of the 62 current staff, four new ones are to become partners in the fall. There are 11 family members now with the firm.

"I really believe we've become an institution in this city," says Mr. McGarry, who once turned down $39 million for the business, "and I don't want to do anything to betray that."

ROD MACIVOR, THE OTTAWA CITIZEN

File photo from the 1979 Diefenbaker funeral as his casket was carried by members of the RCMP from the main entrance of the Parliament Buildings shows a young Brian McGarry on far right. At $500,000, the Chief's funeral was the most expensive in Canadian history.

McGARRY   **HULSE**

Prominent funerals

PRIME MINISTERS

Mackenzie King (1874-1950)
Lester B. Pearson (1897-1972)
John Diefenbaker (1895-1979)

GOVERNORS-GENERAL

Roland Michener (1900-1991)
Jules Léger (1913-1980)
Vincent Massey (1887-1967)
Georges Vanier (1888-1967)

OTHER NOTABLES:

Tommy Douglas, NDP leader, (1904-1986)
Stanley Knowles, NDP MP, (1908-1997)
David Lewis, NDP leader, (1909-1981)
Brian Dickson, Supreme Court chief justice, (1916-1998)
John Sopinka, Supreme Court justice, (1933-1997)
Bora Laskin, Supreme Court chief justice, (1912-1984)
Eugene Forsey, senator, (1904-1991)
Charlotte Whitton, Ottawa mayor, (1896-1975)
Brian Smith, Slain CJOH sports broadcaster, (1940-1995)

At a meeting with The Loewen Group, Vancouver, 1995: Brian McGarry, Ken Bagnell, Joan Sun McGarry, and John Turner. Ken is a dear friend who sat on the Loewen Board, as did John Turner, after serving as Canada's seventeenth prime minister.

The Loewen Group.

China's grave concern

McGARRY SEES HUGE OPPORTUNITY IN LAND-STRAPPED FAR EAST

IT'S ONE of the few virtually risk-free investments you could make in the Far East.

And while entrepreneurs interested in profiting from the development of the so-called booming "tiger" economies of Asia have traditionally also been prepared to assume a high risk, Brian McGarry has demographics on his side, and his numbers are rock solid.

McGarry has spent the last four years preparing to expand the operations of his family-run funeral home operation, Hulse, Playfair and McGarry, into China.

McGarry, who leaves July 30 for a 10-day business trip to Shanghai, beams with excitement as he describes the business opportunities in this particular emerging market.

China's population, now estimated at one billion, is so immense there's little space to devote to traditional earth burials, and the government is encouraging people to cremate their deceased relatives. An astronomical number of 10 million Chinese die every year, and the nation-wide cremation rate is about 33%.

Compare those figures to Ontario, with only 65,000 deaths per year, of which Hulse, Playfair and McGarry might handle 1,600. The company employs 57 and grosses about $6 million annually.

"When you put that in perspective, that's one-third of the population of Canada that dies in China every year," says McGarry, whose mission is to bring North American embalming practices and cremation technology to China, in a joint-venture with the government of the People's Republic.

McGarry, a regional councillor who has twice been named the local businessman of the year, admits it may seem unusual that he's so enthusiastic about the expansion of what many consider a morbid business. "It's no different than anyone else. They're selling widgets and I'm promoting crematoriums," McGarry said.

The opportunity lies in forging partnerships with the state-owned crematoriums, which are both overwhelmed and extremely low-tech, and emit unhealthy levels of pollutants into the air. McGarry plans to tout what he says is the state-of-the-

art cremation system in North America, the so-called "Power-Pak 2" System, manufactured by the Florida-based Industrial Equipment and Engineering Co. "Insert the case, set the controls, and cremation is completed automatically," says the company's glossy promotional flyer.

In addition, embalming techniques common in the west are almost non-existent in China, except for at the funerals of high-profile government officials.

As a result, western funeral service operations have identified an extremely under-serviced and potentially highly-lucrative market. But the prospect of cutting deals with the only surviving Communist superpower on the planet, which also happens to control one-fifth of the world's population, is daunting for even the most sophisticated international business people.

To help break through the red-tape, McGarry has recruited Joan Sun, a 28-year-old bright, personable former Chinese national tour guide whom McGarry met at a conference

CHINA BOUND: Brian McGarry sees huge potential for his funeral business in China.

— FILE PHOTO

'It's no different than anyone else. They're selling widgets and I'm promoting crematoriums'

---

in China he attended in 1993.

McGarry brought Sun to Canada, sponsored her through the Humber College Funeral Service Education program, and the native Mandarin speaker now directs the funerals of the local Chinese community while she plans the operation's Asian expansion.

Sun admits the funeral service business is held in low-regard in China, and says her family thinks she's "crazy".

"I am not a bit ashamed of this business. I think it's a very honorable profession, although not a glamorous one," says Sun.

An economics graduate of Hangzhou University, Sun is providing

cultural and market analysis and interpretation, as well as plenty of business and government contacts for McGarry, all critical for navigating China's immense and sometimes corrupt bureaucracy.

For example, McGarry started researching Beijing, China's seat of government, as a starting point for the venture, but Sun steered him instead toward Shanghai, the country's business centre. Although the country's cremation rate is only 40%, statistics show there are about 100,000 cremations — about 95% of all deaths — annually in the city of 13 million.

"Our government has encouraged people to use cremation instead of earth burial to save the land for the living, not the dead," said Sun.

It's a given the Chinese government will have a majority control of the joint-venture, which McGarry hopes will be undertaking as many as 15,000 cremations per year in Shanghai alone by the year 2000, at a cost of $170 per cremation.

And while monthly incomes of Chinese workers as low as $50 to $85

may make that out of reach for many ordinary workers, in Shanghai it's not unusual to take home salaries as high as $400.

"The numbers of people in itself will dictate the market will do well. It's not like McDonald's, which has to market hamburgers," McGarry said.

The numbers look good, but there's more at stake than just economics in any business venture, and McGarry, a politician, can't ignore the country's poor track record on human rights.

McGarry, a member of the Canada-China Friendship Society, came under fire earlier this year for helping bring a photo exhibit celebrating the Chinese takeover of Hong Kong to regional headquarters.

But McGarry says he's simply following the lead of Prime Minister Jean Chretien, who led a Team Canada expedition to Asia in 1994.

Foreign Affairs says Canada currently does nearly $8 billion in two-way trade with China each year. China is Canada's fourth trading partner after the U.S., Japan, and the U.K., but still only accounts for 1.3% of all Canadian exports. The Canadian government is aiming to boost two-way trade to the country to $20 billion by the year 2000.

"We believe if we engage the Chinese in an open dialogue, we will make more headway on the issue of human rights than if we practice a policy of isolationism," said Sanjeev Chowdhury, a spokesman for the Department of Foreign Affairs.

McGarry says he doesn't condone human rights abuses, and believes the introduction of capitalism and modern technology will help open up the political system.

"I see a sincere attempt to change, whether we're talking about human rights, or we're talking about modernization," McGarry said. "I have no regrets for going in and I have no regrets for staying. That doesn't mean I have to agree with everything that's going on there."

Even Sun acknowledges there are serious problems in her home country's system. "We're not encouraged to speak freely or criticize the government," she understates.

And for critics who say Canada's business ventures in China put profits before people, McGarry responds: "I don't think there's a lot of money to be made for Hulse, Playfair and McGarry. It's more the challenge of putting modern funeral techniques in the People's Republic of China. That's my business. You just take the opportunity that's in front of you."

HELPING EASE PAIN

WAYNE CUDDINGTON, THE OTTAWA CITIZEN

Joan Sun McGarry, wife of Brian McGarry, chief executive of Hulse Playfair & McGarry, is heading to China for a couple of weeks to teach folks the finer art of being a funeral director.

Adding a dose of civility to funerals in China

An Ottawa director is heading back to her homeland to give a keynote speech on the art of providing delicate customer service, **Jennifer Campbell** writes.

China's funeral industry has come a long way since the days — not even a decade ago — when families would wait in line to approach a clerk at a wicket, present a death certificate and discuss insert-name-here style arrangements.

While the wicket concept is fading, the service is still not up to Western standards. But Ottawa's Joan Sun McGarry will try to fix that when she delivers the keynote address at the Shanghai International Seminar on Funeral Service, hosted by the Shanghai Civil Affairs Bureau.

Ms. Sun McGarry came to Canada nine years ago from China to study North America's funeral business practices. She studied at Humber College before starting an internship at Hulse Playfair & McGarry. She had planned to take her expertise back to her native China, but she ended up marrying Brian McGarry, the firm's chief executive,

and joining the family business as a funeral director. These days she frequently deals with clients from the Asian community.

Most of the seminar's delegates will be from Asian countries, although business people from Britain, France, Germany, Italy and the U.S. are also expected.

"It's very flattering to be invited to speak," Ms. Sun McGarry said.

Standards of service for funerals in China is low partly because of the volume of funerals the government-run operations must process. While Shanghai sees 98,000 deaths per year, a city the size of Ottawa averages 5,000.

In her address, Ms. Sun McGarry has been asked to speak about two topics: state funerals, for which Hulse Playfair & McGarry is known in Canada, and standards of quality.

"Partly because of population in China, it is very diffi-

cult to offer very personalized, highly focused service as we do here," she said. "For a long time, it functioned like an industrial process. It was almost as if you were buying a train ticket or having your licence renewed."

By contrast, in North America, clients are invited into comfortable rooms, offered tea or coffee, and given as much time as they need by a professional funeral director.

The meeting kicks off a three-day relationship between funeral home and client.

Still, today in Shanghai, the ticket counter look is a thing of the past, she said. But 10 years ago, the industry just didn't understand the concepts. "The service was not attentive," she said.

Embalming isn't common in China and the existing techniques are still crude, said Mr. McGarry. But, with the push for more attentive service, there's a keen interest in learning North American techniques.

Now settled and committed to staying in Canada, Ms. Sun McGarry is finishing her second year of Queen's University's executive MBA program.

Although Brian's wife, Joan Sun McGarry, will not take any credit for it, she has assisted in bringing twenty-first-century funeral standards to her homeland of China. 2002.

Brian McGarry and Eleanor Milne, Dominion Sculptor. Eleanor is renowned for her stone carvings in the Centre Block; we are honoured to have a glass carving of hers in our Central Chapel depicting Charles Hulse, Keith Playfair, and Brian McGarry. 2006.

Paul Couvrette.

Two of the McGarrys' very best friends, Laureen and Rachel Harper, with Brian and Sheetza McGarry. Laureen and Rachel were strong supporters in Brian's unsuccessful bid for a federal seat in 2008. Lesson learned: stick to the municipal level, where he served the city of Ottawa for twelve years, as councillor of the Regional Municipality of Ottawa–Carleton and trustee and chair of the Ottawa Board of Education. 2008.

Barry Schwerdfeger.

Brian McGarry, Sheetza McGarry, Rachel Harper, Laureen Harper, and Joan Sun McGarry. 2010.

Barry Schwerdfeger.

Sheetza McGarry interviewing former prime minister Jean Chrétien at his law office. Sheetza, along with her good friend Rachel Harper, were assigned a school project to interview a great Canadian. Rachel chose her dad, while Sheetza chose Mr. Chrétien. Both young ladies got top marks! 2010.

Jean-Marc Carisse.

Joan Sun McGarry and Grace Yin with John Baird, Minister of Foreign Affairs, in John's Parliament Hill office. Joan, in addition to assisting McGarry Family Chapels with Asian families and financial affairs, has her own firm, CanadaChina Business Consulting Inc. Grace is a director of Canada–China Inbound Tour Accreditation. John is a guy who gets things done. 2011.

Courtesy of the Office of the Minisgter of Foreign Affairs.

Brian McGarry, Patrick McGarry, and Sharon McGarry.
Michelle Valberg.

THE PARTNERS

HULSE, PLAYFAIR AND MCGARRY

Charles Hulse*	Keith Shaver*	Doug Kennedy*
Percy Hulse*	Laird Barclay*	Tom Flood
Keith Playfair*	Alex Caldwell*	Patrick McGarry
Maurice Hulse*	Brian McGarry	Don Renaud
Keith Campbell*	André Robert*	Robin McGarry*
George Schaef*	Guy Gagné*	Brett McGarry
Cliff Lloyd*	Sharon McGarry	Erin McGarry

LAND DEVELOPMENT PARTNERS

Barry Schwerdfeger	Robert Belton
Stacey Streng	Justine Koopman

*(* indicates former partner)*

STATE FUNERALS

STATE FUNERALS

Assisted by Hulse, Playfair & McGarry

1950	Prime Minister Mackenzie King
1967	Governor General Vincent Massey
1967	Governor General Georges Vanier
1972	Prime Minister Lester B. Pearson
1979	Prime Minister John Diefenbaker
1980	Governor General Jules Léger
1984	Supreme Court of Canada Chief Justice Bora Laskin
1991	Governor General Roland Michener
1998	Supreme Court of Canada Chief Justice Brian Dickson
2000	Prime Minister Pierre Trudeau
2002	Governor General Ramon Hnatyshyn
2007	Supreme Court of Canada Chief Justice Antonio Lamer

2011   Leader of the Official Opposition Jack Layton
(Hulse, Playfair & McGarry provided a supporting role to Heritage Canada and Rosar-Morrison Funeral Home, Toronto.)

FUNERALS WITH STATE INVOLVEMENT

Assisted by Hulse, Playfair & McGarry

1927	Pilot Lieutenant J. Thad Johnson, U.S. Air Force
1986	Tommy Douglas, former premier of Saskatchewan, founder of the CCF (NDP)
1997	Supreme Court Justice John Sopinka
1997	Stanley Knowles, Canadian parliamentarian (CCF/NDP), renowned advocate for social justice
2005	Sergeant Ernest Alvia "Smokey" Smith, last surviving Canadian recipient of the Victoria Cross

GENERAL STORE PUBLISHING HOUSE

499 O'Brien Road, Box 415
Renfrew, Ontario, Canada K7V 4A6
Telephone 1.613.432.7697 or 1.800.465.6072
www.gsph.com

ISBN 978-1-897508-53-4

Design and formatting: Magdalene Carson
Printed and bound in Canada

Library and Archives Canada Cataloguing in Publication
McGarry, Brian, 1943-   From paupers to prime ministers : a life in death / Brian McGarry
Contents: v. 1. The story. v. 2. The album.
ISBN 978-1-897508-45-9 (v. 1 pbk).--ISBN 978-1-926962-49-8 (v. 1 bound)
ISBN 978-1-897508-53-4 (v. 2)
    1. McGarry, Brian, 1943-. 2. Hulse, Playfair and McGarry Ltd.--History. 3. McGarry Family Chapels Inc.--History. 4. Funeral homes--Ontario-- Ottawa--History. 5. Death care industry--Ontario--Ottawa--Biography. I. Mahar, Paul, 1972- II. Title.
HD9999.U54H85 2012   338.7'61363750971384   C2010-905601-9

Cover photographs:
Front:
The casket of Pierre Trudeau leaving the Hall of Honour, 2000: *Jean-Marc Carisse*
Back, from left to right:
Charles Hulse and Keith Playfair: *Yousef Karsh.*
Brian McGarry: *Jean-Marc Carisse.*

To order more copies, please contact
GENERAL STORE PUBLISHING HOUSE

CREDITS FOR PRESS CLIPPINGS

16 "Massey Dies in UK." Image and article: The Canadian Press.

17 "A Quiet Farewell to Massey." Images and article: City of Ottawa Archives/MG011/p.2.

18 "Canadian mourn statesman-leader: Pearson funeral Sunday." Article: Southam News Service. By permission of the *Ottawa Citizen*.

18 "'Rare man'—Trudeau: Tributes pour in." Article: The Canadian Press.

18 "One-eyed Mike umpire-baiter." Article: The Canadian Press.

18 Lester was no name for an aspiring pilot." Article: The Canadian Press.

19 "Twilight Farewell to Mike." Image: The Canadian Press / Peter Brigg. Article: By permission of the *Ottawa Citizen*.

26 "John Diefenbaker dead." Image of John Diefenbaker and article: City of Ottawa Archives/MG011/p.1.

26 "John Diefenbaker dead." Image: "Faithful McAndy watches his master depart": The Canadian Press / Rene Pierre Allain. Article: City of Ottawa Archives/MG011/p.1.

32 "Three-day state rites set for 'remarkable son.'" Article: By permission of the *Ottawa Citizen*.

40 "Legendary crusader for social justice Stanley Knowles dies at 88: 'A great parliamentarian.'" Image: The Canadian Press / Tom Hanson. Article: QMI Agency.

41 "Saint Laid to Rest." Image and article: QMI Agency.

53 "A Quintessential Canadian: Ray Hnatyshyn 1934–2002." Images: Brigitte Bouvier and Rod MacIvor. Article: By permission of the *Ottawa Citizen*.

63 "Malak Karsh 'had a smile for everyone.'" Image: David Chan. Article: By permission of *Ottawa Citizen*.

65 "Stanfield remembered for decency, integrity." Images: The Canadian Press / Fred Chartrand; Wayne Cuddington / *Ottawa Citizen*. Article: By permission of the *Ottawa Citizen.s*

66 "Sharp: Great example of public service to the end of his life." Images: The Canadian Press / Tom Hanson; Wayne Cuddington / *Ottawa Citizen*. Article: By permission of the *Ottawa Citizen*.

70 "Four killed in townhouse fire tragedy." Image and article: By permission of the *Ottawa Citizen*.

70 "Wakefield couples killed, 'pillars of community' gone." Image and article: By permission of the *Ottawa Citizen*.

80 "'All of us knew them as our brothers.'" Image: Wayne Cuddington / *Ottawa Citizen*. Article: By permission of the *Ottawa Citizen*.

109 "Senators' suite spot." Image: Julie Oliver / *Ottawa Citizen*. Article: By permission of the *Ottawa Citizen*.

110 "On the Team." Image and article: QMI Agency.

138 "The Funeral Home to Ottawa's Elite." Image: Rod MacIvor /*Ottawa Citizen*. Article: By permission of the *Ottawa Citizen*.

130 "China's grave concern." Image and article: QMI Agency.

131 "Adding a dose of civility to funerals in China." Image: Wayne Cuddington / *Ottawa Citizen*. Article: By permission of the *Ottawa Citizen*.

All proceeds from this book will be donated
to the Ottawa Regional Cancer Foundation
and the Queensway-Carleton Hospital.

FROM PAUPERS
TO PRIME MINISTERS

A LIFE IN DEATH

BRIAN M^cGARRY

GSPH

FROM PAUPERS
TO PRIME MINISTERS

A LIFE IN DEATH

Brian McGarry. Fifty years in funeral and cremation services.
May 1, 1962–May 1, 2012.

Jean-Marc Carisse.

TABLE OF CONTENTS

With thanks

Following the example of our good friend Rabbi Reuven Bulka's "kindness week," we wish to thank the community for their kindness in supporting Joan through her recent and unexpected cancer surgery. Thanks to the Queensway-Carleton Hospital, Dr. Centazza, and her team. Thank you to the Civic Campus, Dr. Moultan, Dr. Zwicker, Dr. Alsaffar, and their teams at the Neurosciences Clinic in A2 and the Short-Term Rehab Unit.

Our appreciation to many individuals who came forward to lend a hand: Mary-Ellen and Kelly Schwerdfeger; Melanie Yasinski; Laureen and Rachel Harper; Charlyne and Michael McNeil; Brett McGarry and Anne Tardiff and Carolyn Coté. In addition, the kindness of parents from Elmwood School and Rockcliffe Park Public School will be remembered.

Finally, thank you to our colleagues. We now fully understand what Charles Hulse and Keith Playfair meant when they said, "We are all family." In return, we will keep their example and our continued commitment to maintain Hulse, Playfair & McGarry Family Chapels/Cremation Centres family-owned.

Joan Sheetza Brian

THE OTTAWA CITIZEN

Thursday, 28 February 2008